Cromosys Publication

Teach Yourself Autodesk 3ds Max

NIRANJAN JHA SHOWMAN

Founder - Niranjan Jha Showman

Education and Technology Research Center

Patankar Park, Nallasopara (W), Mumbai. +91-9561450045

Education, Technology, Publication, Healthcare, Newsmedia, Realtor, Filmmaking

www.facebook.com/cromosys

+91-9561450045
Learn Advanced Skills
And Get Job Instantly
GERMAN
Python
FRENCH
C++
SPANISH
Java
ENGLISH
HTML5
RUSSIAN
CSS
JavaScript
Cromosys
Education and Technology Research Center
Nallasopara (W), Mumbai

Learn Web Programming
Demo-Class Free
HTML
CSS
React
JavaScript
Typescript
Bootstrap
Cromosys
20 Years of Experience
Nallasopara (W), Mumbai
+91-9561450045

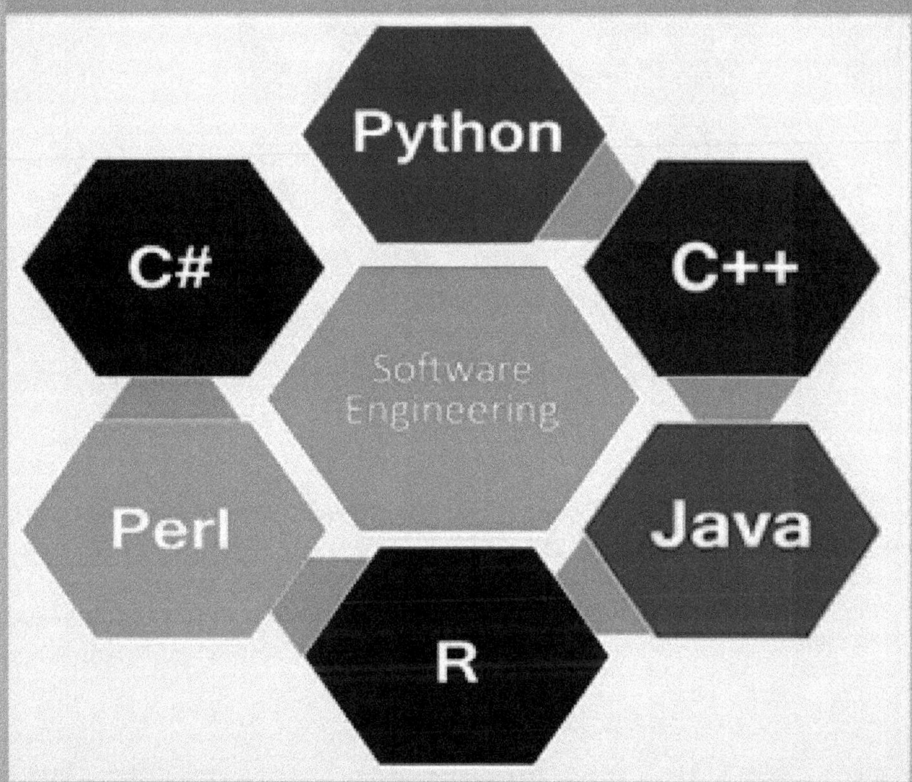
+91-9561450045
Learn Software Engineering
Demo-Class Free
Python
C#
C++
Software
Engineering
Perl
Java
R
Cromosys
20 Years of Experience
Nallasopara (W), Mumbai
+91-9561450045

25 Years of Experience
Learn Visual Multimedia
Animation VFX
Movie Editing
Game Development
Cromosys
+91-9561450045
Education and Technology Research Center
Nallasopara (W), Mumbai
www.facebook.com/cromosys

Jobs Available
For Candidates Who Know

German
French
Spanish

Vacancy in Germany, France, Spain

For Hospitality, Engineering, IT Sector

With Free Visa, Airfare and Accommodation

Cromosys
Education and Technology Research Centre
Nallasopara (W), Mumbai
+91-9561450045
20 Years of Experience

+91-9561450045
Foreign Languages Institute
German, French, Spanish
Basic and Advanced - All Levels
3 x 6 = 18 Courses
FRANCHISE
Business Offer
Teaching Materials Provided
We have 1 Million Students Globally
Great Income Assured
Global Exposure
Cromosys
20 Years of Experience
Nallasopara (W), Mumbai
+91-9561450045

Book: Teach Yourself Autodesk 3ds Max
Author: Niranjan Jha Showman
Publisher: Cromosys Publication
ISBN: Acquired
Category: Computer Education
Sub-category: 3D modeling and Animation

Preface

Cromosys Publication's **Teach Yourself Autodesk 3ds Max** book is an optimal quality guide to the beginners and advanced learners of 3ds Max. We are the leading eBook publisher of languages and technology. Our research and education center working for last fifteen years has made tremendous effort to simplify the learning of Max, and so, we assure you that this book will walk you through in a very simple way in your entire course of learning. Whether you are using 3ds Max 8 or the newer version, this book will make you a master of it in just one month. The tutorials in the chapters will lead you step-by-step giving pictures of every move and will help you create and design models from scratch, not like other books that tell you to copy things and make shallow editing. We do not encourage the misguidance of this kind at all as learning Max is not a child's play. Today's world is the world of 3d design and animation, and everyone wants to create a moving, talking, and interacting visual expression. You may be interested in creating an animation movie, a game, architectural design, editing the content of a film, earning a way to Hollywood, or impressing your loved one. Max can serve all your purposes, as it does all the works of this kind. The lessons conceived and prepared by us will let you start from real basic in easy steps making it amazing, astonishing, and exhilarating for you. And soon you will feel that you've got a new horizon to present your imagination. It's cool, simple, and sublime!

Niranjan Showman, the author of this and fifteen others eBooks available online, is the founder of Cromosys Corporation. His dedication in technological and linguistic research is significantly known to the millions of people around the world. This book is the creation of his avowed determination to make the learning of Max easy to the people. After you install this program on your system, you just have to follow the instructions doing the same on your computer, and you will see that you are quickly learning everything. Just an hour of practice per day, and in a month of time you'll get a lot of knowledge, tips and tricks to work with this software. This is an unmatchable unique book of its kind that guarantees your success. The lessons are magnificently powerful to bring you into the arena of design and animation. Since it is the need of time, the people around the world have been sharpening their knowledge to be good in it. The still-image creation software like CorelDraw, Photoshop, and Illustrator are where you create the pictures of your choice, but when you wish to present them in three dimensions with animation, there you need Max. What Max does, no other software can do. It is totally different. For instance, if you want to design a car showing its all dimensions, do you think any other software can do that? No, absolutely not. Only Max can do that and it can do in just a few minutes of time, and so it is proven that Max is must for a 3D designer or an architectural engineer like you.

Now you may need to ask us whether it is necessary to learn still-image creating software like CorelDraw, Photoshop, and Illustrator before starting Max. For that, our answer is "no", not at all. Whether you know about any of this software or not, you can still start learning Max. From the year of 2013, with the industrial growth, the accurate and profound knowledge of Max has influenced zillions of minds; therefore we conceived the idea of making this book a guideline for those who want to be perfect in 3ds Max starting from real basic. One more thing is important to mention here that nobody can learn Max playing around it, and even nobody can play around also. People do learn other software like Microsoft Paint, CorelDraw and Photoshop in casual efforts, but Max cannot be cowed down in that manner. It is dynamic, resolute, vivid and vivacious and that's why we salute Max a thousand times. If you dare to be inattentive, you'll experience your own fall as you'll understand nothing of it. It needs your attentive, continuous, controlled and patient efforts. Don't get carried away from the first lesson and start doing irrelevant things of your own as it happens because of the vivaciousness of this software. You'll burst into laughter or start dancing when you'll see your drawing moving in all dimensions, but believe me, there would be still more to learn. For your technical information, Max is one of the most important software for Multimedia and Animation, and also for architects.

Cromosys, our education and technology research center, saving human efforts from being wasted, is committed to help you gain profound and contemporary knowledge. The world growing with density has brought enormous opportunity to animation talents irrespective of their geographical boundaries. We strongly believe this book is useful for the people working for art and design, Web creation, media houses, entertainment world, and obviously for those who love animation. After you start the lesson, you don't need to worry about anything but just follow each and every step carefully. This eBook is designed to fulfill the instant need of learners in a very economical way, as it is easy to find on internet and affordable to buy and share. Cromosys, our path-breaking pioneer training institute for Computer Courses, English Speaking, Mass Communication, Foreign Languages, and Competition Coaching, is dedicated to enlightening human mind with educational endeavors, and we are doing the same for last successful fifteen years. And recently we have come up with 'Worldwide Online Teaching System' for languages and technology. We not only hope but believe that your success is in your hand now, as this book will take you miles ahead in your expectation. We always respect the views and comments of readers, so for any communication with regards to assistance, enquiry or collaboration, we are always there at your reach as it helps us improve our quality.

Niranjan Jha Showman
Founder: Cromosys Corporation
Web: facebook.com/cromosys
Contact no.   +91-9561450045
Email address: cromosys@yahoo.com
Facebook link: www.facebook.com/niranjanshowman

Books by the same author: Teach Yourself Maya, Teach Yourself Adobe Flash, English Voice Accent and Pronunciation, Teach Yourself Spanish, Teach Yourself French, Teach Yourself German, English Word Power, Dynamic Grammar of English, English Dictionary of Modern Slang, English Accent and Diction

Cromosys
Education and Technology Research Center
Education, Technology, Publication, Healthcare, Realtor, Filmmaking
Nallasopara (W), Mumbai, India

Caution: All the writing works that include all the educational, non-educational books, novels, and articles of the writer Niranjan Jha, are the published content of his registered magazine FACE OFF - Inventing Truth, which carries registration no. MAHENG12112/13/1/2009-TC and the endorsement no. 3244 28/5/2009 with the Ministry of Information and Broadcasting, Govt. of India. Any plagiarism in this regard will attract strict legal action. Any further publication of any of these books requires his written permission. Copyright certificate of this book is attached at the end of this book.

Lesson 1
Introduction

After you install 3ds Max (version 8 or newer) in your system, you can go ahead and open this program. You'll the screen as shown in picture 1.1. Before you start drawing anything, I need to tell you the basic things of this screen.

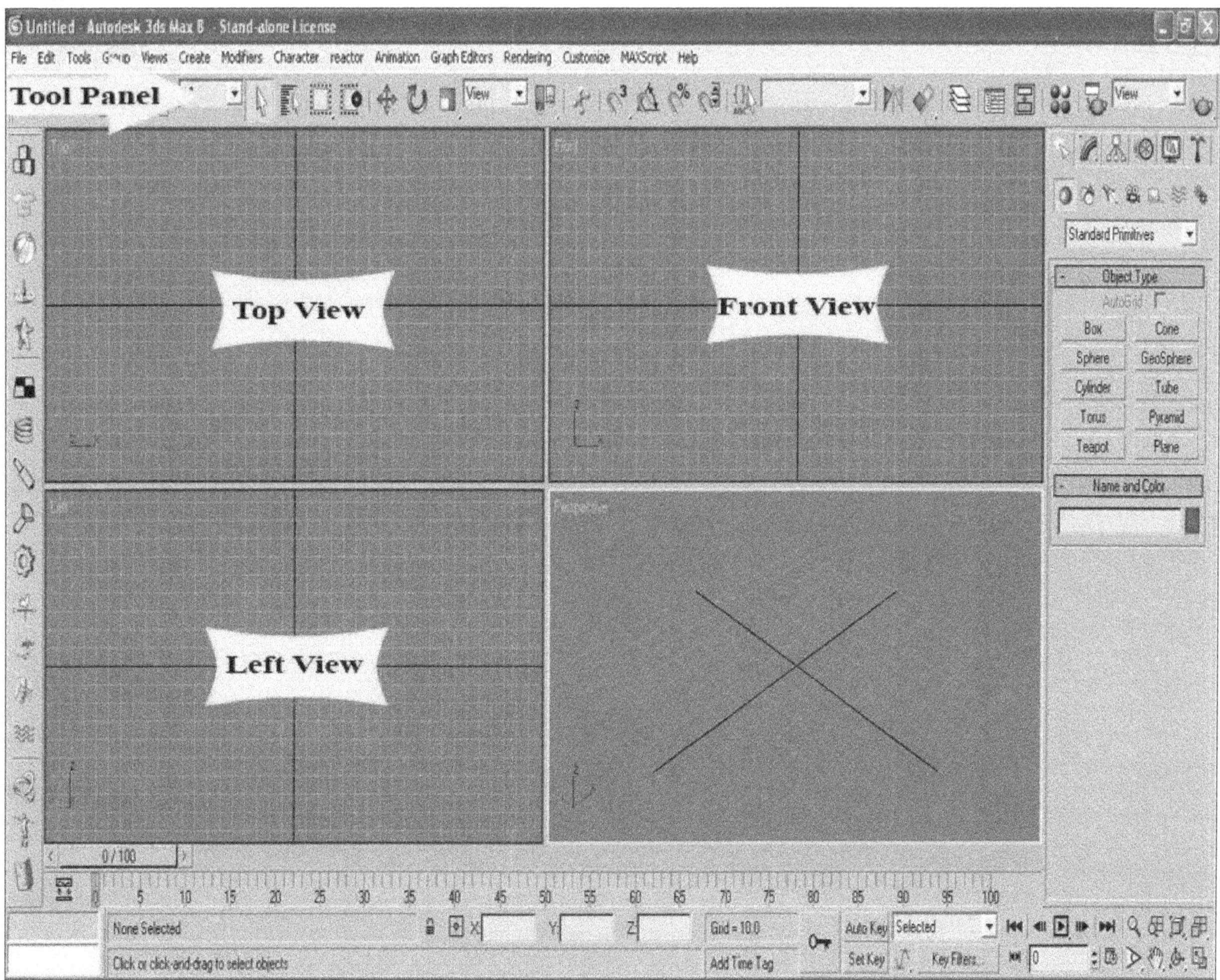

Picture 1.1

First of all I tell you how you can work with Max. It begins with the imagination that you should have in your mind of what you want to create. Then you select a raw object from Max Stock (that I'll explain you later), and drag the object in Top, Front, Left, or Perspective viewport of the screen as shown above. Then you select the tool from Tool Panel and model the object deciding which part (Top, Front, or Left) of the object needs to be edited. The Perspective viewport lets you see the actual image as a final output of your design. Remember that whatever you draw in Max, it creates it's all the three dimensions (Top, Front, or Left), and that dimensions you see when you rotate the image in Perspective viewport, or for a better view you export the image to .DWF format and open in Autodesk DWF Viewer that is already installed in your system with Max. Seeing your image in DWF Viewer will blow you off. The purpose of this lesson is to give you a taste of what Max can do. This soaring view of the software from 20,000 feet is intended to show you the big picture before you delve into the details. It exposes you to the most common features—including many new features— and whets your appetite for the more in-depth lessons to follow.

Creating an Image

1. You're going to model a character and so you'll create only the basic shape that includes the body and head of it. For convenience, let's call this character ImageOne. Go to Menu bar and click on Create> Standard Primitives> GeoSphere. You see that on the right panel GeoSphere button is activated. Select the Top viewport and drag to create a GeoSphere object with a Radius of about 60. You can adjust (enter) the Radius value below Parameters in the same right panel. Drawing in Top viewport means you want the object to be at the top of everything.

2. Right-click the GeoSphere object in Top viewport, select Convert To> Convert to Editable Poly from the pop-up quadmenu.

3. Click the (+) sign of Editable Poly which is down below Modifier List in right panel which is called Command panel, (don't click the radio button of Modifier List), and select the Polygon subobject mode. Put a checkmark in Ignore Backfacing option in the Selection rollout to make sure the polygons on the reverse side of the sphere aren't selected.

4. Now drag over the five topmost polygons (with mouse pointer) in the Top viewport. You'll see that the polygons turn red when selected (dragged over). Select the Extrude tool in the Edit Polygons rollout, and drag five selected polygons upward in the Top viewport a short distance to create the character's neck. See picture 1.2 for help. Then click the Extrude button to exit Edit mode.

5. Hold down the Ctrl key, and click to select two polygons on the upper-front of the sphere in the Front viewport. Then use the Extrude tool to drag out some arm stubs. As you're in Front viewport, you've to drag upward to draw arms. After it is done, click Perspective viewport and keep on pressing the down arrow key on keyboard to let the ImageOne go smaller in size to be shown entirely. Your Perspective view may look like picture 1.3. Don't worry about the color this time as you may change it anytime later.

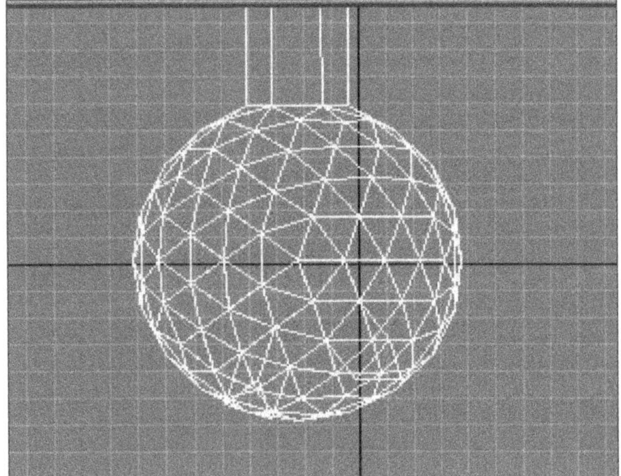

Picture 1.2

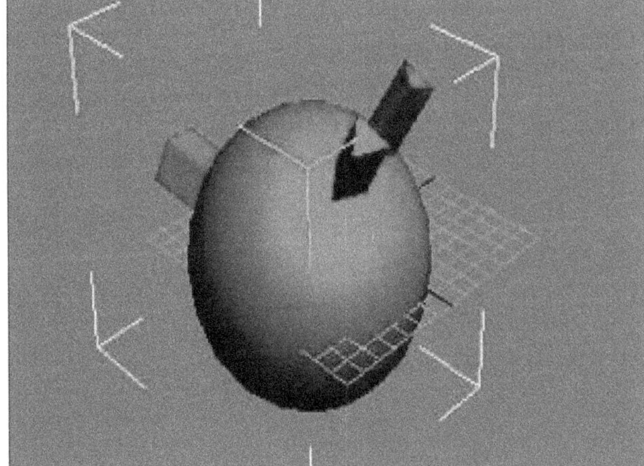

Picture 1.3

6. Select five lower polygons in the same Front viewport and repeat the extrude steps to extrude stubs for both legs. Then go to Left viewport, and select one polygon and extrude it for the tail. Save this project with the name ImageOne.max (in .max format) and then go to Export and select Save as type Publish to DWF (.DWF format). Open .DWF file in Autodesk DWF Viewer and you may see the result as shown in picture 1.4. Use Orbit tool and other tools (below menu bar) in DWF Viewer to see ImageOne's all the three dimensions.

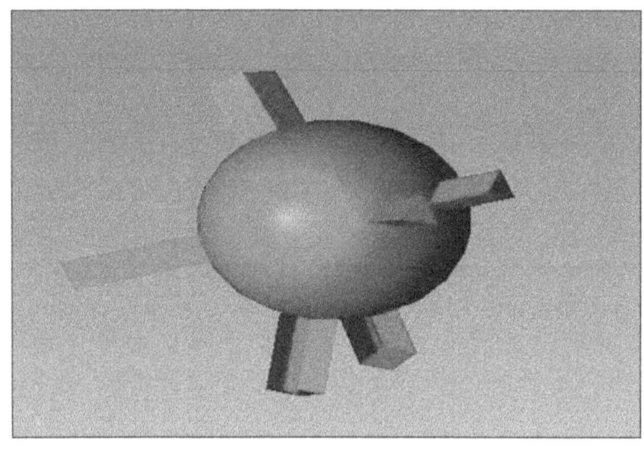

The result of this project doesn't look like a valid character, but it provides a good starting point that you can enhance with details like a face, arms, and legs. The body of ImageOne character is a simple GeoSphere with extruded limb stubs. I believe it is a good start and I assure you that what you're going to learn in next lesson is just logical, not difficult and not at all impossible. Max has brightened the career of millions in the world, and it may do yours as well. Don't worry about anything but just keep moving. How know how hard it is, but only hard things pay you well.

Picture 1.4

Lesson 2
Modeling ImageOne's Head

Now we're going to make the head of ImageOne. The head consists of two puffy cheeks and large ellipsoid eyes. We'll create these general shapes by attaching several primitive objects together.

1. Open the same ImageOne.max file that you saved in lesson 1. Use <u>Select and Rotate</u> tool and <u>Select and Move</u> tool from the main toolbar to bring the head of ImageOne upfront in Front viewport as shown in picture 1.5. Make sure that after rotating and moving down, the picture in your Front viewport looks similar to what is shown in picture 1.5.

2. To create and attach the head, select Left viewport, go to Create> Extended Primitives> Capsule, and drag in the Left viewport to the left-side to create a Capsule object with a Radius of about 18 and a Height of around 80. Give light yellow color (or any color you want) to it. Select Perspective viewport and use <u>Select and Move</u> tool to place the capsule on the neck of ImageOne, as shown in picture 1.6.

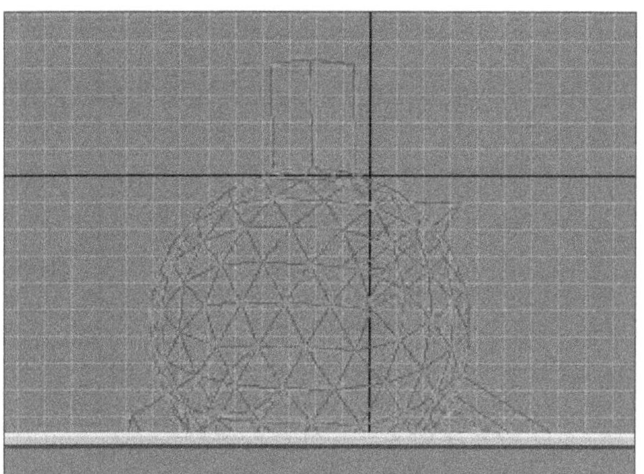

Picture 1.5

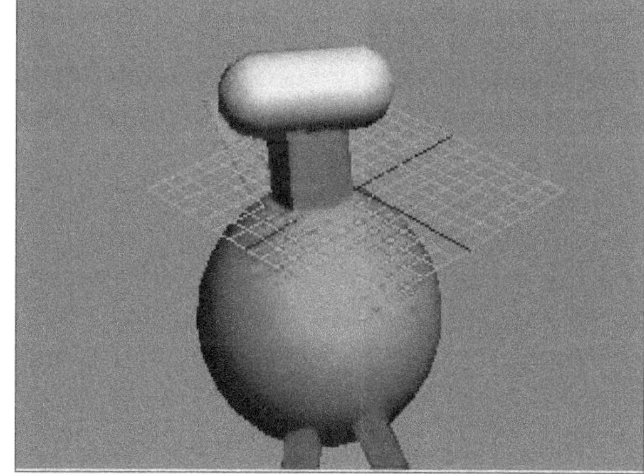

Picture 1.6

3. Select Front viewport and go to Create> Standard Primitives> GeoSphere, and drag in the Front viewport above the Capsule object to create a GeoSphere object with a Radius of about 15. We use Front viewport because we want the new object to be drawn at the front of ImageOne. Use Move tool to fix it rightly above the Capsule and apply black color. It's going to be the eye of the image. Select the <u>Select and Uniform Scale</u> tool from the main toolbar, and drag the GeoSphere object's Y-axis up to make

it long. You have to use <u>Move</u> and <u>Rotate</u> tools quite often and also work in Front, Left, and Perspective viewport (one at a time) simultaneously to bring out better result.

4. Select Front viewport, pick up Move tool, hold down the Shift key, and drag the new GeoSphere to the left in the Front viewport to create a copy of the GeoSphere. In the Clone Options dialog box, select Copy and click the OK button. With Move tool selected, click on Left viewport and fix the Clone of the eye at the right place, and the right place you can judge when you look at the Perspective viewport while working on Left viewport. Now they should look like a pair of eyes in your Perspective viewport as shown in picture 1.7 below.

5. Select Front viewport, go to Create> Standard Primitives> GeoSphere menu command to create a third GeoSphere in front of the Capsule and the existing GeoSphere objects. The two elongated GeoSphere form the eyes, and the newest GeoSphere is the nose, and the Capsule object is the cheeks. You can give this newest GeoSphere (nose) red color. Use Move tool in Left viewport to fix it at right place. Remember that moving object in a different viewport solve the radius problem automatically. As we are reaching the end of this lesson, so your Perspective view should look like the picture 1.8 shown below.

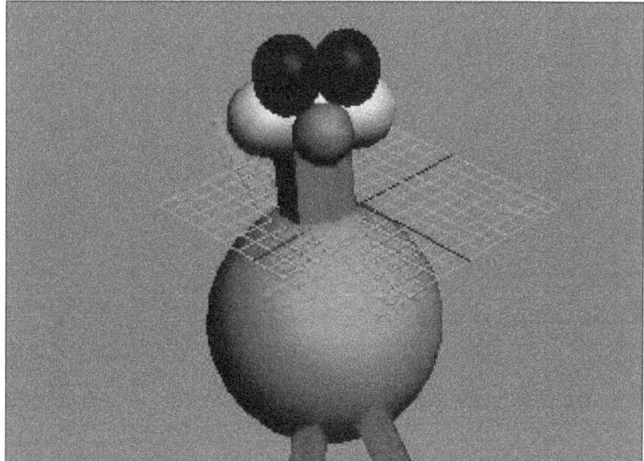

Picture 1.7   Picture 1.8

6. Select the nose GeoSphere and click on Create> Compound Objects> Boolean button. Choose the Pick Operand B button in the Pick Boolean rollout, and click the Capsule object (don't worry if Capsule disappears). Make sure the Move option is selected below the same Pick Operand B, and double click the Parameters rollout button and choose the Union option in the Operation section of the same Parameters rollout. It brings the Capsule back and combines the two objects into one and removes the interior polygons. The only problem with Boolean command is that the objects in union lose their own colors, but don't worry about the color this time as you can learn about editing colors in Lesson 4.

7. Click the Select button in the main toolbar; click the Boolean button again, select the Pick Operand B button, and choose the eye GeoSphere. Then repeat this step for the other eye. With the Move tool, position the head over the neck stub and repeat the Boolean union step to attach the head to the body object. We need to have the entire ImageOne combined in Union with Boolean command for its next edit. We still need to work on the arms, feet, and tail, but for now we seem to be getting ahead. The result of this project may look similar to what you see in picture 1.8 (but entirely in red color). Save this file now and you can export and see this in DWF Viewer.

Lesson 3
Editing the body
In this lesson we have to model the body of ImageOne. The body is still too spherical, and the limbs are too blocky. To edit the body part, follow these steps:

1. Open the same .max file that you saved in Lesson 2. Adjust the image in Left viewport using Select, Move, and Rotate tools so that you can edit the body. You can use middle mouse button to zoom in and zoom out. After adjusting the image for next move, your Left viewport should look similar to the picture 1.9, and your Perspective viewport similar to 2.0.

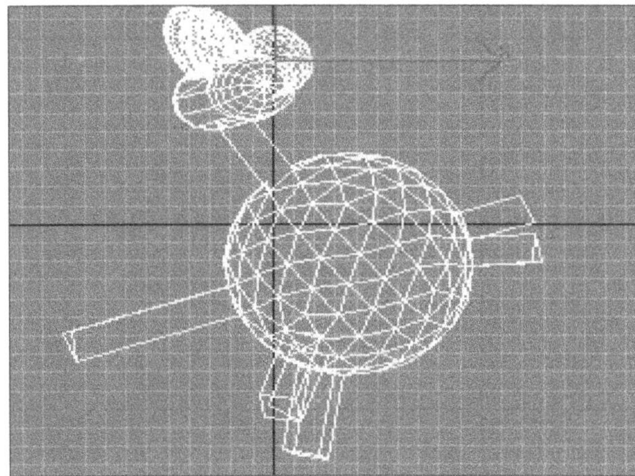

Picture 1.9

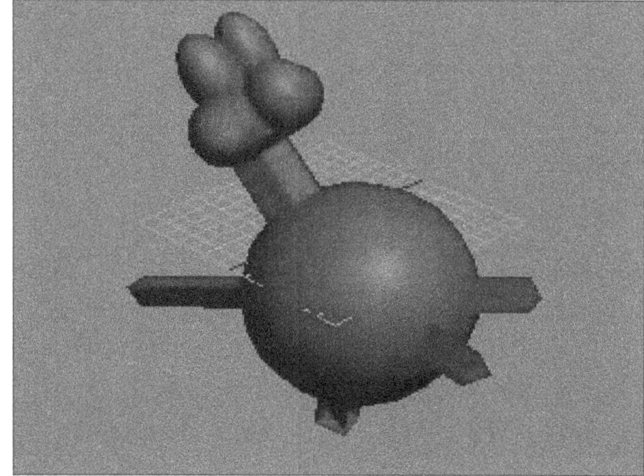

Picture 2.0

2. Right-click the body, and convert it to an Editable Poly object. Then select the Polygon subobject mode, and select all the body polygons (Ctrl + click) below the neck (don't select neck). Use the Scale and Move tools to scale the body in the Y- and Z-axes. You have to deform the body in order to make it broad, as shown in picture 2.1. To view your creation while editing, you can uncheck polygon button and use Move and Rotate tools in Perspective viewport, but make sure you select back the same Polygon subobject mode for editing further.

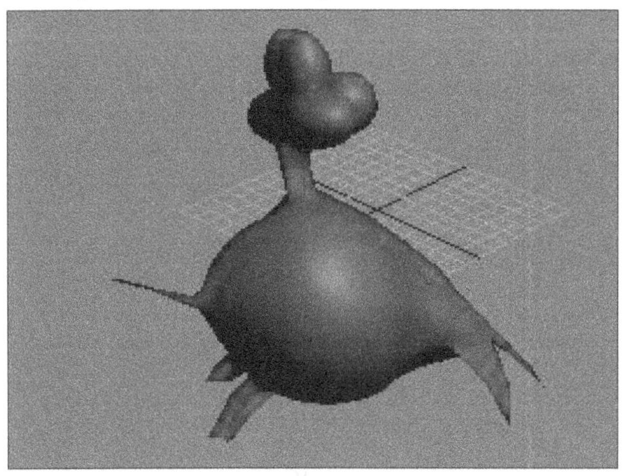

Picture 2.1

3. Open the Soft Selection rollout, and enable the Use Soft Selection option. Set the Falloff value to 35. Drag over the arms in the Left viewport, and then scale, rotate, and move them to pull the body out away from the rest of the body. Repeat this for the tail and legs, adding more deformation to the body. It requires your skill here. Your final result should look like the picture 2.1.

4. In Polygon subobject mode, drag over each front arm independently and rotate the arms downward to act more like front feet. You may see that moving the front arms down causes some polygons in the front of the body to overlap. To fix this problem, select the problem areas and click the Relax button in the Edit Geometry rollout several times. It may take hours and several attempts of yours to reach the final result.

5. With the deformation looking much better and not so spherical, you can apply an MSmooth to smooth some areas. Click the MSmooth button to apply a mesh smooth over the entire character. The process of deforming the body gives the creature an organic look. With the body deformed and looking more organic and animal like, the character is starting to look like a critter you'd find in the deep woods.

Lesson 4
Adding materials
Now from here onwards you would feel that you're embracing Max. In this lesson you would add materials that complete the coloring of ImageOne's nose, eyes, and feet. For this, we use the Multi/Sub-Object material.

1. Select Rendering, click Material Editor, and click Standard button in the right-middle side of the new window. Now double-click the Multi/Sub-Object from the list, select <u>Keep old material as sub-material</u> and click the OK button.

2. In the Multi/Sub-Object Basic Parameters rollout, click the <u>Set Number </u>button which is in the middle, enter the number 4 in the box and hit OK. Then click (single click) the first Sub-Material, change the Diffuse color to white, and enter the number 90 in <u>Specular Level</u> box and number 10 in Glossiness. Then click the Material ID Channel button (small blue color 'O' button) once and that sets the Material in channel 1. Click the Go Forward to Sibling button (black right-arrow button) to access the second sub-material. The easiest way to scroll the main toolbar is to drag with the middle mouse button.

3. Change the Diffuse color to black, set the Specular Level to 94, the Glossiness value to 70, and the Material ID Channel to 2. Then click the Go Forward to Sibling button again to access the third sub-material.

4. Change the Diffuse color to black, the Specular Level to 76, the Glossiness value to 20, and the Material ID Channel to 3. Then click the Go Forward to Sibling button again to access the fourth sub-material.

5. Change the Diffuse color to light brown and the Material ID Channel to 4. Click the Go to Parent button, and drag the material from its sample slot onto the ImageOne character in Perspective viewport. Then close the Material Editor.

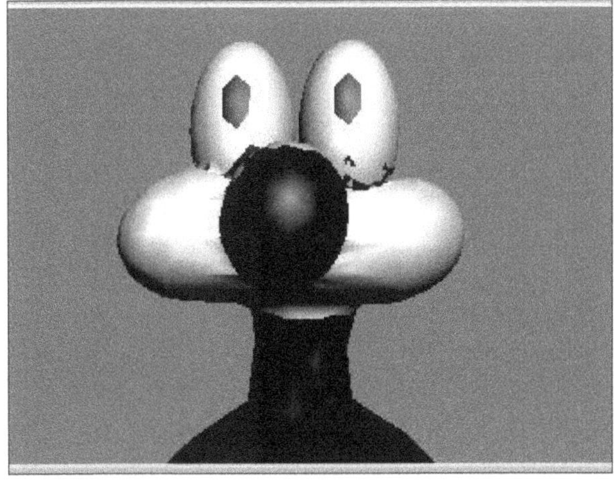

Picture 2.2

6. Select the Polygons subobject mode, disable <u>Ignore Backfacing</u> from Selection rollout, select all the character polygons, and set the Material ID to 4 in the Polygon Properties rollout. Then select the polygons that make up the eyes (for that you can make the image view large using Uniform Scale tool that works when you disable Polygon subobject mode), and set the Material ID to 1 (this time Polygon subobject mode should be enabled). Select the front feet, and set the Material ID to 2. Finally, select the nose, and set the Material ID to 3.

7. In the Soft Selection rollout, disable Soft Selection. Press and hold the <u>Rectangular Selection Region</u> button in the Tool Panel and choose the Circular Selection Region from the flyout. In Polygon subobject mode, select a group of polygons in the center of each eyeball, and set the Material ID to 3. That's all. You see that adding materials helps to define the various character parts. See the result in picture 2.2. Adding materials differentiates the various body parts clearly.

Lesson 5
Adding Fur
Now we're going to add the fur using the Hair and Fur modifier. The benefit of fur is that it covers lots of the details we don't need to paint.

1. Select the body object of ImageOne with Select tool, choose Modifiers> Hair and Fur> Hair and Fur WSM. Now you'll see several hairs displayed in the viewports.

2. Click (+) sign of Hair and Fur in the right panel below Modifier List, select Polygon subobject (under Hair and Fur, not under Editable Poly). Now drag with mouse pointer over entire ImageOne's body excluding the head, front feet, and the soles of the back feet. Then click the Update Selection button in the Selection rollout. This removes the hair from the unselected areas.

3. Click the Tools rollout, click the Load button to open the Hair and Fur Presets dialog box, and double-click the Fuzzybrown.shp thumbnail. In the General Parameters rollout, set the Hair Count to 30000, the Scale value to 20, the Root Thickness to 1.0, and the Tip Thickness to 0.3.

4. Although the hair has been added to the character, it isn't visible until the scene is rendered. So select Perspective viewport, go to Rendering (from Menu Bar)> Render> and click the Render button in the Render dialog box. It will take at least five minutes of time to render on your system and then you may see the rendered image similar to picture 2.3.

Picture 2.3

Adding hair to the ImageOne character hides lots of detail so we don't have to model or texture. If you think the hairs are looking less on the body, you can increase the number in Hair Count and do Rending again. Save this as JPEG format and after you close rendering dialog box, don't forget to save the original file in .max format. Now you're ready to dive into the features of Max program. Keep moving, don't give up. After doing one or two lessons more, you'll feel bliss in your life!

Lesson 6
Creating a forest backdrop
Now we're going to add a background image to make it look like ImageOne is in forest. To add a scenic backdrop, get a JPEG picture of forest and save it in your computer. Now follow these steps:

1. Go to Rendering> Environment and enable the Use Map check box. Click the Environment Map button labeled "None." The Material/Map Browser dialog box appears.

2. In the right pane of the Material/Map Browser is a list of materials and maps. Double click the Bitmap item. The Select Bitmap Image File dialog box opens.

3. Locate the forest picture in your computer. Click Open to load the background image. When loaded, the image's filename appears on the button in the Environment panel. Click the red X button to close the Environment panel.

Picture 2.4

4. You can rotate and drag ImageOne down in the Perspective viewport so that it should look at the right place in the forest. Now go to Rendering> Render and when the rendering process finishes, you'll see the result similar (or better if you add more hair to ImageOne in Lesson 5) to the picture 2.4.

So it was your first footstep into Max by which you learnt about modeling characters, and basic modeling features including extrude, smooth, and relax. You also learnt how to apply materials to a character to define body parts, and add fur to a character. And finally you came to know about adding a background image and rendering the scene. Now you have to get ready for more advanced challenges the software lies ahead.

Lesson 7
Learning the main Tool Panel

At the top of the Max screen you see Menu Bar and Tool Panel (or Toolbar). The options of Menu Bar will be explained later when you'll do hands-on projects, but the Toolbar is explained to you now so that you can understand the functionalities of Max. Picture 2.5 shows Max Toolbar with options alphabetically numbered that are explained below.

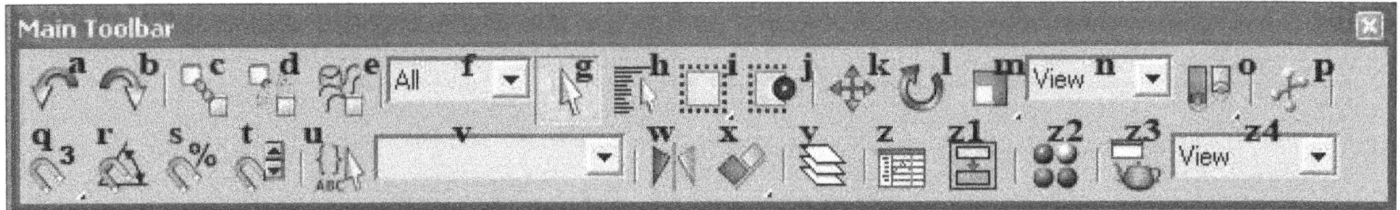

Picture 2.5

A (Undo) - Removes the last performed command.
B (Redo) - Brings back the last command that was undone.
C (Select and Link) - Establishes links between objects.
D (Unlink Selection) - Breaks links between objects.
E (Bind to Space Warp) - Assigns objects to be modified by a warp.

F (Selection Filter) - Limits the type of objects that can be selected.
G (Select Object) - Chooses an object.
H (Select by Name) - Opens a dialog box for selecting objects by name.
I (Rectangular Selection) - Determines the shape used for selecting objects. It has five options in it.
J (Window/Crossing Toggle) - Specifies whether an object must Toggle be crossed or windowed to be selected.
K (Select and Move) - Selects an object and allows positional translations.
L (Select and Rotate) - Selects an object and allows rotational transforms.
M (Uniform Scale) - Selects an object and allows scaling transforms using different methods. It has three options in it.
N (Reference Coordinate List) - Specifies the coordinate system used for transforms.
O (Pivot Point Center) - Specifies the center about which rotations are completed.
P (Select and Manipulate) - Selects an object and allows parameter manipulation.
Q (Snap Toggle 2D) - Specifies the snap mode. 2D Snap Toggle 2.5D, snaps only to the active
Snap Toggle 3D (S) construction grid, 2.5D snaps to the construction grid or to geometry projected from the grid, and 3D snaps to anywhere in 3D space. It has three options.
R (Angle Snap Toggle) - Causes rotations to snap to specified angles.
S (Percent Snap) - Causes scaling to snap to specified percentages.
T (Spinner Snap Toggle) - Determines the amount a spinner value changes with each click.
U (Edit Named Selection) - Opens a dialog box for creating and managing selection sets.
V (Named Selection List) - Lists and allows you to select a set of named objects.
W (Mirror Selected Objects) - Creates a mirrored copy of the selected object.
X (Align, Quick Align, Normal Align, Place Highlight, Align to Camera, Align to View) – It has six options.
Y (Layer Manager) - Opens the Layer Manager interface where you can work with layers.
Z (Open Curve Editor) - Opens the Function Curves Editor.
Z1 (Open Schematic View) - Opens the Schematic View window.
Z2 (Material Editor) - Opens the Material Editor window.
Z3 (Render Scene Dialog) - Opens the Render Scene dialog box for setting rendering options.
Z4 (Render Type List) - Selects the area or objects to render.

Learning Command Panel

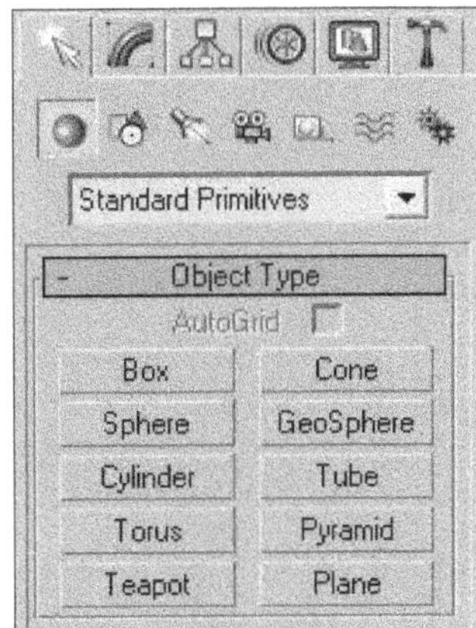

The Command Panel is located to the right of the viewports along the right edge of the interface that you already used a few times before. It includes six separate panels accessed via tab icons. This is where the object parameters, settings, and controls are located. The Command Panel is split into six panels, each accessed via a tab icon located at its top. These six tabs are Create, Modify, Hierarchy, Motion, Display, and Utilities. Pressing the Ctrl+~ keyboard shortcut closes all open dialog boxes. Pressing the same keyboard shortcut again reopens the dialog boxes that were previously closed. The picture 2.6 A shows the Command Panel. You will be using this panel quite often in coming lessons. The lessons of this book (as it should be) are interconnected to each other, so you are advised not to jump off but go step by step.

Picture 2.6 A

This was the interface elements for Max. Understanding the interface is one of the keys to success in using 3ds Max. Max includes a variety of different interface elements. Among the menus, toolbars, and keyboard shortcuts, several ways to perform the same command exist.

Creating an apple

Picture 2.6 B

Here's what will thrill you – creating an apple, wow! Why, to eat? No, but you can create a real-looking apple in a minute. (1) Click on Torus text button under Standard Primitives, select red color and draw it in Perspective viewport. (2) In Parameters rollout set Radius 1 value to 14, Radius 2 to 13. (3) Using Uniform Scale tool you can give it a better look. (4) Click GeoSphere under Standard Primitives, pick up green color and draw a small object in Top viewport to place it at the top. (5) Select the green object in Perspective viewport, click Modify tab in Command Panel, and set Radius to 2. With Uniform Scale tool pull it up. Your apple should look as good as the picture 2.6 B.

Configuring viewports

The viewports are the main elements of Max interface. The four main viewports make up the bulk of the interface and are the one place where scene objects are visible. Learning to control and use the viewports can make a huge difference in your comfort level with Max. The viewports are powerful and have numerous settings that you can use to provide thousands of different ways to look at your scene.

What is 3D Space

In today's world we live in 3D space. If we stop and think about it, 3D space is natural to us. For example, consider a filing cabinet with four drawers. Within each drawer, you can stuff papers in the front, back, or sides, as well as in the drawers above or below. These positions represent three unique directions. Now the computer screen, which is inherently 2D where you understand top and bottom and left and right and have a little notion of above and below, how would you represent 3D objects on it? For this what Max does is that it presents several views, called viewports, of the scene. A viewport is a small window that displays the scene from one perspective. These viewports are the windows into Max's 3D world.

Max includes several keyboard shortcuts for quickly changing the view in the active viewport including T (Top View), B (Bottom View), F (Front View), L (Left View), C (Camera View), $ (Spotlight View), P (Perspective View), and U (Isometric User View). Pressing the V key opens a quad-menu that lets you select a new view.

Increasing the size of Perspective viewport

From the next lesson we're starting extensive design and modeling, and for that you may have understood that most of the works you have to do in Perspective viewport. Now you would be trying to find out the ways of making Perspective viewport big. One of the several ways to increase the size of your viewport is to click and drag the viewport borders. Dragging on the intersection of the viewports resizes all the viewports.

You can also enter Expert Mode by choosing Views> Expert Mode. It maximizes the viewport space by removing the toolbars, the Command Panel, and most of the Lower Interface Bar. With most of the interface elements gone, you'll need to rely on the menus, keyboard shortcuts, and quad-menus to execute commands. To re-enable the default interface, click the Cancel Expert Mode button in the lower right corner. Sometimes, a Max artist requires a larger monitor as well.

Lesson 8
Creating a spring

You can create a lot of objects using Command Panel. The Parameters tab gives you the control of editing the object to your choice. We're starting with a simple object spring. Now you get the chance to learn the things by imagining, doing, and exploring into Max. Here are the steps to follow:

1. Now as your Perspective viewport is bigger, you can go ahead and click the filter button of Command Panel and select Dynamic Objects.

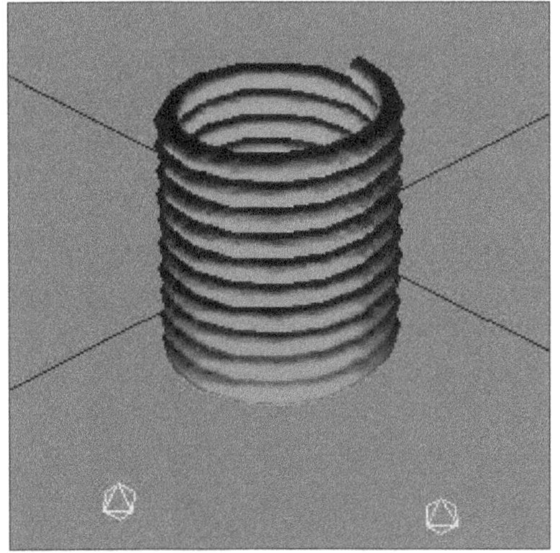

2. Select Spring tab under Object Type, and draw a spring in Perspective viewport. Under Name and Color tab, select the color green, under Spring Parameters set Height: 25, Diameter: 20, Turns: 10. You're free to use Move, Rotate, and Uniform Scale tools to give the Spring a better look. If anytime you lose the Spring Parameter tab, clicking Modify tab at the top of Command Panel will bring it back.

3. Click Lights tab in Command Panel and select Omni. Set two Omni light spots by clicking at the bottom-left and bottom-right of the Spring. Picture 2.7 shows the Spring with Omni light spots at the bottom.

Picture 2.7

Saving it as .max format can let you edit further and exporting to .DWF lets you view in DWF Viewer. The next lessons will make you familiar with Camera, Motion, and Mental Ray effect in Command Panel.

Lesson 9
Creating a tree

In this lesson you can create a tree with two objects of Command Panel. The steps are quite easy. Let's go ahead with this:

1. In Command Panel select AEC Extended (or go by clicking Create in Menu bar), click Foliage and select the Generic Palm tree from Favorite Pants tab. Click and drag it in Perspective viewport, use common editing tools (Move, Rotate, and Uniform Scale) to give it a right shape and size.

2. Select Standard Primitives in Command Panel, pick up Box, and draw a box at the bottom of the tree, as shown in picture 2.8. Give it a light black color and put it at right place using Move tool. That's it! Like this, you can create some more objects picking up Torus Knot from Extended Primitive, Walls from AEC Extended, and Point Surf from NURBS Surfaces. Many objects of this kind are also used for architectural structures.

Picture 2.8

Modeling a head

Now you're going to create a 3D image of a human head which requires some skill. Following the steps mentioned below will help you create and modify the image.

1. First go ahead and open a New Scene by clicking File> New. When the new scene is open, you can select Create> Systems> Biped and drag a long Biped image in Perspective viewport. This time common editing tools (Transformation tools) will not work.

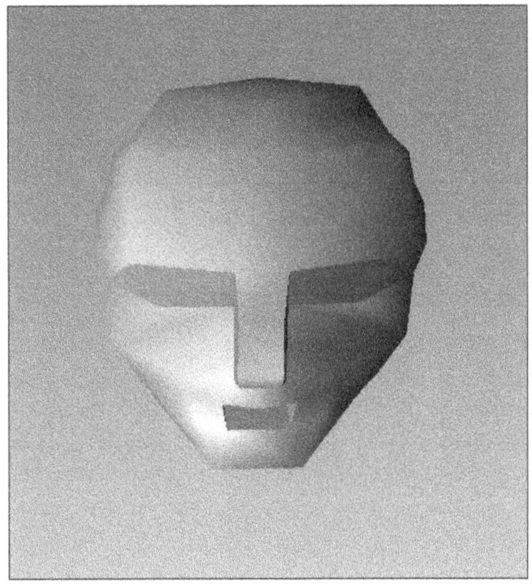

2. Pick up Select Tool, hold Ctrl key down and click to select all the parts of the body except head. With Select Tool still active, right click on the selected area of the image and choose Convert to> Convert to Editable Poly.

3. Click Modifier List filter tab under Command Panel and select DeleteMesh. If any part of the body except head is left in the viewport, you can drag over it to select and hit DeleteMesh again.

4. Select head with Select Tool, right-click on it, go to Convert to> Convert to Editable Mesh and choose Element (not Polygon) by clicking the + sing of Editable Mesh. Use common editing tools (Move, Scale, and Rotate) to make the head bigger and place it in the middle.

Picture 2.9

5. Pick up Select Tool; choose Polygon under Editable Mesh, and holding Ctrl key down select four polygons under the nose of the head to create the mouth. Then click Edit Geometry rollout and select Extrude.

6. In the Extrude box, enter -2 (minus two) and hit enter. Select upper polygons of the head by dragging over them and use Scale Tool to scale them up. You can do some more editing if you wish. At the end, your image may look like the picture 2.9.

Lesson 10

The viewports in Max

Now you would like to know the importance of viewports that include Front, Back, Top, Bottom, Left, and Right. Max starts up with the Top, Front, and Left orthographic viewports visible. The top-left corner of the viewport displays the viewport name. The fourth default viewport is a Perspective view. You can see the model from a different direction in each viewport. If you want to measure an image's length, you could get an accurate measurement using the Top or Left viewport, whereas you can use the Front and Left viewports to measure its precise height. So, using these different viewports, you can accurately work with all object dimensions.

Viewport Navigation Control

You can control the viewport you're working in using the Viewport Navigation Control buttons. The standard viewports show you several different views of your current project, but within each viewport you can zoom in on certain objects, pan the view, or rotate about the center of the viewport. To zoom, pan, and rotate the default views, you need to use any of the eight buttons located at the bottom-right corner of the window. The active viewport is always marked with a yellow border. The keyboard shortcut for each button is listed in parentheses next to its name.

Viewport Navigation Controls Buttons
Picture 3.0 shows the set of Viewport Navigation Controls Buttons with their sub-options. You'll need to use these buttons which are located at the bottom-right corner of Max screen.

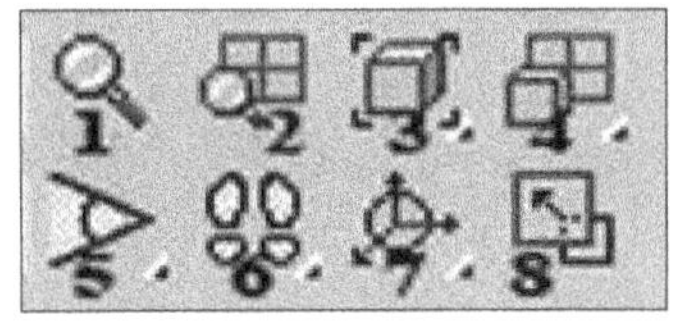

1. Zoom (Alt+Z) - Moves closer to or farther from the objects in the active viewport by dragging the mouse.
2. Zoom All - Zooms in to or out of all the viewports simultaneously by dragging the mouse.
3. Zoom Extents (Ctrl+Alt+Z) - Zooms in on all objects or just the selected object until it fills the active viewport.

Picture 3.0

4. Zoom Extents All (Ctrl+Shift+Z) - Zooms in on all objects or just the selected object until it fills all the viewports.
5. Field of View, Region Zoom (Ctrl+W) - The Field of View button (only available in the Perspective view) controls the width of the view. The Region Zoom button zooms in to the region selected by dragging the mouse.
6. Pan (Ctrl+P or I), Walk Through - Moves the view to the left, to the right, up, or down by dragging the mouse or by moving the mouse while holding down the I key. The Walk Through feature moves through the scene using the arrow keys or a mouse like a first-person video game.
7. Arc Rotate (Ctrl+R) - Rotates the view around the global axis, selected object, or sub-object by dragging the mouse.
8. Min/Max (Alt+W) - Toggle Makes the active viewport fill the screen replacing the four separate viewports. Clicking this button a second time shows all four viewports again.
The thing you need to take care of is that when one of the Viewport Navigation buttons is selected, it is highlighted yellow, and you cannot select, create, or transform objects at that time. You have to right-click in the active viewpoint to select object mode.

Walking through a view
The Walk Through button, found as a flyout button under the Pan button, allows you to move through the scene in the Perspective or Camera viewport using the arrow keys or the mouse just as you would if you were playing a first-person computer game. When this button is active, the cursor changes to a small circle with an arrow inside it that points in the direction you are moving. The Walk Through feature includes several keystrokes for controlling the camera's movement. The arrow keys move the camera forward, left, back, and right (or you can use the W, A, S, and D keys). You can change the speed of the motion with the Q (accelerate) and Z (decelerate) keys or with the [(decrease step size) and] (increase step size) keys. The E and C keys (or the Shift+up or Shift+down arrows) are used to move up and down in the scene. The Shift+Spacebar key cause the camera to be set level. Dragging the mouse while the camera is moving changes the direction in which the camera points.

Rotating a view
Rotating the view can be the most revealing of all the view changes. When the Arc Rotate (Ctrl+R) button is selected, a rotation guide appears in the active viewport. This rotation guide is a circle with a square located at each quadrant. Clicking and dragging the left or right squares rotates the view side to side; the same action with the top and bottom squares rotates the view up and down. Clicking within the circle and dragging rotates within a single plane, and clicking and dragging outside of the circle rotates the view about the circle's center either clockwise or counterclockwise.

Controlling camera and spotlight views
You can set any viewport to be a camera view (C) or a spotlight view ($) if a camera or a spotlight exists in the scene. When either of these views is active, the Viewport Navigation Control buttons change. In camera view, controls for dolly, roll, truck, pan, orbit, and field of view become active. A light view includes controls for falloff and hotspots.

Creating a fish
The uniqueness of this book is that it helps you draw everything from scratch rather than telling you to download something half-made from somewhere and do some shallow editing in that. I know how frustrating it would be, and you'll go haunted looking for the starting steps. Here is your start:

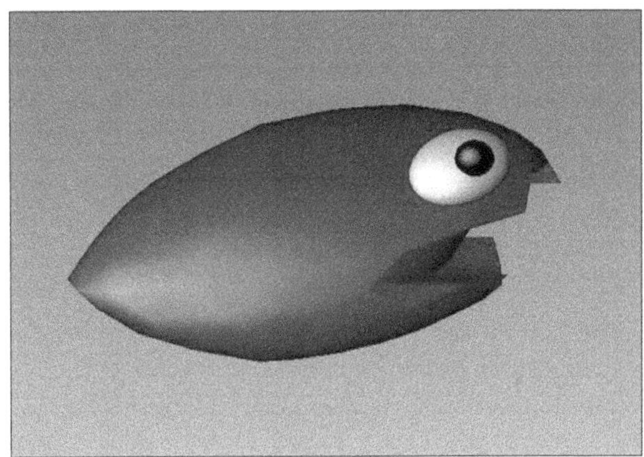

1. Select GeoSphere from Standard Primitives and drag to draw it in Perspective viewport. Right-click on it, select Convert to Editable Poly, and select Polygon from Modifier List dropdown.

2. Select some upper polygons using Fence Selection Region tool of Rectangular Selection Region and press Relax button (under Edit Geometry) a few times to make the object go flat from the top. You can do the same from the bottom also. Try using Uniform Scale to make the object look like the body of a fish.

Picture 3.1

3. Now draw another GeoSphere in the Left viewport so that it comes in front of the body object. Give it white color to make it look like an eye-socket. Draw one more GeoSphere in Left viewport, give it black color and place it in the middle of the white object. You can use Zoom option in Left viewport to be sure about the radius of the two objects. You may have to zoom and work in all the viewports simultaneously to adjust the radius of white and black objects. Don't worry about the time it takes. You can view your advancement in DWF Viewer while working in Max.

4. At last, select some polygons from right-middle in Perspective viewport using Fence Selection Region tool, and use Extrude from Edit Polygons to make the mouth of the fish. Your image should look similar to the picture 3.1. Just keep it in mind that you have to do a lot of practice to be perfect in it.

Lesson 11
Saving changes made with the Viewport
This lesson covers the first part of the Basic Information of Max Interface. As you know that you can have navigation controls in Max. If you get lost in your view, you can undo and redo viewport changes with Views> Undo View Change (Shift+Z) and Views> Redo View Change (Shift+Y). These commands are different from the Edit> Undo and Edit> Redo commands, which can undo or redo geometry changes. You can save changes made to a viewport by using the Views> Save Active Viewport menu command. This command saves the Viewport Navigation settings for recall. To restore these settings, you can use Views> Restore Active Viewport. The Save and Restore Active Viewport commands do not save any viewport configuration settings, just the navigated view.

You saw that the active viewport can be maximized. To increase the size of your viewports the first trick to try is to change the viewport sizes by clicking and dragging any of the viewport borders. Dragging on the intersection of the viewports resizes all the viewports. You can return to the original layout by right-clicking on any of the viewport borders and selecting Reset Layout from the pop-up menu.

The second trick to try is to use the Min/Max Toggle (Alt+W) to expand the active viewport to fill the space reserved for all four viewports. Clicking the Min/Max Toggle (or pressing Alt+W) a second time returns to the defined layout. You can also enter Expert Mode by choosing Views> Expert Mode (Ctrl+X). It maximizes the viewport space by removing the toolbars, the Command Panel, and most of the Lower Interface Bar. To re-enable the default interface, click the Cancel Expert Mode button in the lower right of the Max window (or press Ctrl+X again).

Viewing grids

Grids are helpful in establishing your bearings in 3D space. For the active viewport, the G key turns the grids on and off. The Views> Grids command opens a submenu with the following options: Show Home Grid, Activate Home Grid, Activate Grid Object, and Align Grid to View.

Displaying various viewport items

Next on the Views menu are several commands that control what is displayed in the viewport. If a command is enabled, a check mark appears to the left of the command. The Show Transform Gizmo command displays axes and special handles to move, rotate, and scale the object in different directions. The Show Ghosting command displays the position of the selected object in the previous several frames, the next several frames, or both. The Show Key Times command displays frame numbers along the trajectory path where every animation key is located. The Shade Selected command turns on shading for the selected object in all viewports, and the Show Dependencies command shows any objects that are linked or instanced from a parent object. The Create Camera from View command (Ctrl+C) creates a camera and positions it to match the current view. The Add Default Lights to Scene command converts the default lights to actual light objects in the scene. This feature lets you start with the default lights and modify them as needed. The Windows Copy Command (Ctrl+C) doesn't work in Max.

Disabling and refreshing viewports

If your scene gets too complicated, you can experience some slow-down waiting for each viewport to be updated with changes. In that case the first option to try is to disable a viewport. You can disable a viewport by right-clicking on the viewport's name and selecting the Disable View menu command from the pop-up menu, or you can press the keyboard shortcut, D. When a disabled viewport is active, it is updated as normal; when it is inactive, the viewport is not updated at all until it becomes active again. Disabled viewports are identified by the word "Disabled," which appears next to the viewport's name in the upper-left corner. Another trick to increase the viewport update speed is to disable the View> Update During Spinner Drag menu option. Changing parameter spinners can cause a slowdown by requiring every viewport to update as the spinner changes. If the spinner is changing rapidly, it can really slow even a powerful system. Disabling this option causes the viewport to wait for the spinner to stop changing before updating. Sometimes when changes are made, the viewports aren't completely refreshed. This typically happens when dialog boxes from other programs are moved in front of the viewports. If this happens, you can force Max to refresh all the viewports with the Views> Redraw All Views (keyboard shortcut, `) menu command. It makes everything visible again.

Using clipping planes

Clipping planes define an invisible barrier beyond which all objects are invisible. For example, if you have a scene with many detailed mountain objects in the background, working with an object in the front of the scene can be difficult. By setting the clipping plane between the two, you can work on the front objects without having to redraw the mountain objects every time you update the scene. This affects only the viewport, not the rendered output. Enabling the Viewport Clipping option places a yellow line with two arrows on the right side of the viewport. The top arrow represents the back clipping plane, and the bottom arrow is the front clipping plane. Drag the arrows to set the clipping planes. You can quickly turn Viewport Clipping on or off by right-clicking the viewport name and choosing Viewport Clipping from the pop-up menu.

Grabbing a viewport image

It's not rendering, but you can grab an image of the active viewport using the Tools> Grab Viewport. Before grabbing the image, a simple dialog box appears asking you to add a label to the grabbed image. The image is loaded into the Rendered Frame Window, and its label appears in the lower-right corner of the image. I know that you would like to use quite often.

Lesson 12

Importance of Safe Frames

This lesson covers the second part of the Basic Information of Max Interface. Safe Frames provide the guides that can help you see when the scene objects are out of bounds. Completing an animation and converting it to some broadcast medium, only to see that the whole left side of the animation is being cut off in the final screening, can be discouraging. The Safe Frames feature, as shown in picture 3.2 displays some guides within the viewport that show where these clipping edges are.

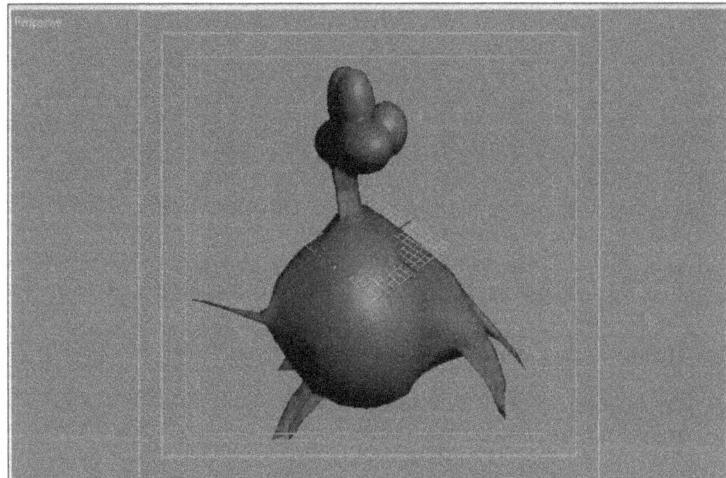

You can quickly enable or disable Safe Frames by right-clicking the viewport name and choosing Show Safe Frame in the pop-up menu (or you can use the Shift+F keyboard shortcut). And you can configure Safe Frames also by right-clicking the viewport name> Configure> Safe Frames. For each type of safe frame, you can set the percent reduction by entering values in the Horizontal, Vertical, or Both fields. The 12-Field Grid option offers 4 × 3 and 12 × 9 aspect ratios. The options in the configuration dialog box are-

Picture 3.2

Live Area: Marks the area that will be rendered, shown as yellow lines. If a background image is added to the viewport and the Match Rendering Output option is selected, then the background image will fit within the Live Area.

Action Safe: The area ensured to be visible in the final rendered file, marked with light blue lines; objects outside this area will be at the edge of the monitor and could be distorted.

Title Safe: The area marked with orange lines where the title can safely appear without distortion or bleeding.

User Safe: The output area defined by the user, marked with magenta lines.

12-Field Grid: Displays a grid in the viewport, marked with a pink grid.

Loading viewport background images

The Views> Viewport Background menu command (Alt+B) opens a dialog box in which you can select an image or animation to appear behind a viewport. The displayed background image is helpful for aligning objects in a scene, but it is for display purposes only and will not be rendered. To create a background image to be rendered, you need to specify the background in the Environment dialog box, opened using the Rendering> Environment. If the background image changes, you can update the viewport using the Views> Update Background Image menu command (Alt+Shift+Ctrl+B).

Loading viewport background animations

The Animation Synchronization section of the Viewport Background dialog box lets you set which frames of a background animation sequence are displayed. The Use Frame and To values determine which frames of the loaded animation are used. Loading an animation sequence as a viewport background can really help as you begin to animate complex motions, like a running horse. By stepping through the frames of the animation, you can line up your model with the background image for realistic animations.

Saving and opening files

In Max, you can save files in .max extension that allows you to open them for editing at a later time. Max also supports files saved with the .chr extension used for character files. In case of opening rendered files, you can also open VIZ Render files that have the .drf extension. Selecting a file and clicking on the plus button opens a copy of the selected file with a new version number appended to its name.

Managing files

The Files panel includes several options that define how to handle files. The first option is to Convert File Paths to UNC (Universal Naming Convention). This option displays file paths using the Universal Naming Convention for any files accessed over a mapped drive. The next option is Backup on Save. When you save a file using the File> Save (Ctrl+S) menu command, the existing file is overwritten. The Backup on Save option causes the current scene file to be saved as a backup (with the name MaxBack.bak in the 3dsmax\autobak directory) before saving the new file. If the changes you made were a mistake, you can recover the file before the last changes by renaming the MaxBack.bak file to MaxBack.max and reopening it in Max.

Another option to prevent overwriting your changes is the Increment on Save option. This option adds an incremented number to the end of the existing filename every time it is saved. This retains multiple copies of the file and is an easy version-control method for your scene files. This way, you can always go back to an earlier file when the client changes his mind. With this option enabled, the MaxBack.bak file isn't used. The Compress on Save option compresses the file automatically when it is saved. Compressed files require less file space but take longer to load. If you're running low on hard drive space, then you'll want to enable this option.

Auto Backup feature

With this feature enabled, Max saves the file in case of system crash. You can select the number of Autobak files to keep around and how often the files are backed up. To set it up, (1) open the Preference Settings dialog box by choosing Customize> Preferences, and click the Files panel. (2) Turn on Auto Backup by selecting the Enable option in the Auto Backup section. (3) Set the number of Autobak files to 2. The backup files are saved to the directory specified by the Configure Paths dialog box. The default is to save these backups to the 3dsmax\autoback directory. You can also select a name for backup files.

This is how it works: If you've set the number of backup files to 2, the interval to 5 minutes, and the backup name to MyBackup, then after five minutes the current file is saved as MyBackup1.max. After another five minutes, another file named MyBackup2.max is saved, and then after another five minutes, the MyBackup1.max file is overwritten with the latest changes.

Importing supported formats

Max can import several different formats, including the following:

- 3D Studio Mesh, Projects, and Shapes (3DS, PRJ, SHP)
- Adobe Illustrator (AI)
- LandXML/DEM/DDF
- AutoCAD (DWG, DXF)
- Alias (FBX)
- Motion Analysis (HTR, TRC)
- Initial Graphics Exchange Standard (IGE, IGS, IGES)
- Autodesk Inventor (IPT, IAM)
- Lightscape (LS, VW, LP)
- StereoLithography (STL)
- Wavefront Material and Object (MTL, OBJ)
- VRML (WRL, WRZ)
- VIZ Material XML Import (XML)

Exporting supported formats

You sometimes export Max objects for use in other programs. For that, you've to go to File> Export. Max can export to several different formats, including the following:

- 3D Studio (3DS)
- Adobe Illustrator (AI)
- ASCII Scene Export (ASE)
- AutoCAD (DWG, DXF)
- Alias (FBX)
- Design Web Format (DWF)
- Initial Graphics Exchange Standard (IGS)
- JSR-184 (M3G)
- Lightscape Material, Blocks, Parameters, Layers, Preparations and Views
- Motion Analysis (HTR)
- Wavefront Material and Object (MTL, OBJ)
- StereoLithography (STL)
- Shockwave 3D Scene Export (W3D)
- VRML97 (WRL)

Though there are many export formats but the Design Web Format (DWF) is an ideal format for displaying your textured models to others via the Web. It creates relatively small files that can be attached easily to an email. The Autodesk DWF Viewer is automatically installed along with 3ds Max. If you want to view the exported files in the viewer, simply enable the Show DWF in Viewer option in the DWF Publish Options dialog box. The viewer includes controls for transforming the model, changing its shading and view, and printing the current view.

Exporting to the Shockwave 3D (W3D) format

Shockwave 3D is an interactive format used by Macromedia's Director Software. The exporter includes an Analysis tool and a Preview window. To export a Max scene to the Shockwave 3D format, you can select File> Export and select the Shockwave 3D format as the File Type in the file dialog box. After you give the file a name and click OK, the Shockwave 3D Scene Export Options dialog box opens. This dialog box contains several options that you can include in the export file, such as Geometry, Animations, Material, Texture maps, Shaders, and Lights. You can also select a camera to use or choose to use the Active Viewport. The Compression Settings for Geometry, Texture, and Animation can be set to different quality settings between 0 and 100, and you can choose to limit the texture size.

Importing vector drawings from Illustrator

A professional designer prefers to use Illustrator to design the company logo. It is an advanced vector drawing Software. When importing vector-based files into Max, only the lines are imported. Max cannot import fills, blends, or other specialized vector effects. All imported lines are automatically converted to Bézier splines in Max that you'll learn in detail from this book.

To import Adobe Illustrator files into Max, (1) you can go ahead and draw some rectangle box in Illustrator and save the file using .AI format. (2) You've to be kind enough for one thing that while saving select Illustrator 8 format instead of the latest Illustrator CS sequel. (3) Open Max, and choose File> Import. Select Adobe Illustrator (AI) as the File Type in the dialog box. Locate the file to import, and click OK. (4) The AI Import dialog box asks whether you want to merge the objects with the current scene or replace the current scene. For our purposes, select the replace the current scene option and click OK. (5) The Shape Import dialog box asks whether you want to import the shapes as single or multiple objects. Select multiple, and click OK. As said earlier, if you've filled colors in the Illustrator drawing, that won't be imported into Max.

Selecting System Units

One of the first tasks you need to complete before you can begin modeling is to set the system units. The system units have a direct impact on modeling and define the units that are represented by the coordinate values. Units directly relate to parameters entered with the keyboard. For example, with the units set to meters, a sphere created with the radius parameter of 2 would be 4 meters across. Max supports several different measurement systems, including Metric and U.S. Standard units. You can also define a Custom units system (I suggest parsecs if you're working on a space scene). Working with a units system enables you to work with precision and accuracy using realistic values.

To specify a units system, choose Customize> Units Setup to display the Units Setup dialog box. For the Metric system, options include Millimeters, Centimeters, Meters, and Kilometers. The U.S. Standard units system can be set to the default units of Feet or Inches displayed as decimals or fractional units. You can also select to display feet with fractional inches or feet with decimal inches. Fractional values can be divided from 1/1 to 1/100 increments.

To define a Custom units system, modify the fields under the Custom option, including a units label and its equivalence to known units. The final option is to use the default Generic units. Generic units relate distances to each other, but the numbers themselves are irrelevant. You can also set lighting units to use American or International standards. At the top of the Units Setup dialog box is the System Unit Setup button. This button opens the System Unit Scale dialog box. This dialog box enables you to define the measurement system used by Max. Options include Inches, Feet, Miles, Millimeters, Centimeters, Meters, and Kilometers. A multiplier field allows you to alter the value of each unit. The Respect System Units in Files toggle presents a dialog box whenever a file with a different system units setting is encountered. If this option is disabled, all new objects are automatically converted to the current units system. The Origin control helps you determine the accuracy of an object as it is moved away from the scene origin. If you know how far objects will be located from the origin, then entering that value tells you the Resulting Accuracy. You can use this feature to determine the accuracy of your parameters. Objects farther from the origin have a lower accuracy.

Enabling AutoPlay

The AutoPlay Preview File setting automatically plays Preview Files in the default media player when they are finished rendering. If this option is disabled, you need to play the previews with the Animation> View Preview menu command.

Enabling ghosting

Ghosting is similar to the use of "onion-skins" in traditional animation, causing an object's prior position and next position to be displayed. When producing animation, knowing where you're going and where you've come from is helpful. Enabling ghosting helps you to produce better animations. Max offers several ghosting options. You can set whether a ghost appears before the current frame, after the current frame, or both before and after the current frame. You can set the total number of ghosting frames and how often they should appear. You can also set an option to show the frame numbers.

Lesson 13
Creating Primitive Objects

From this lesson you're going to restart learning Max. The previous lessons made you acquainted to the practical setting of it and gave the basic information of its interface so that you can get charged to continue learning.

You use primitive objects to do any modeling job in Max. After you create a primitive, you can then bend it, stretch it, smash it, or cut it to create new objects applying additional skills of cloning, grouping, or transforming. The Create menu offers quick access to the buttons in the Create panel which is in Command Panel at the top right of Max window. The picture 3.3 shows the Command Panel with the Create panel clicked (shown). And the picture also illustrates numbered 1 as Create tab, 2 as Category icons with all seven buttons, and 3 as Subcategory dropdown list.

All the objects that you can create using the Create panel you can access using the Create menu.

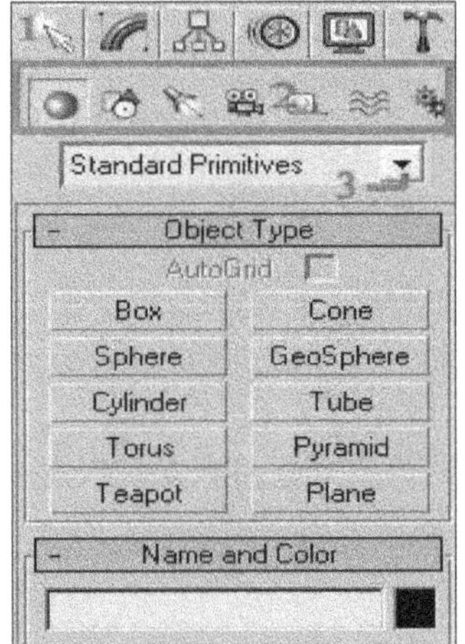

Selecting an object from the Create menu automatically opens the Create panel and selects the correct category, subcategory, and button needed to create the object. The creation of all default Max objects, such as primitive spheres, shapes, lights, and cameras, starts with the Create panel.

Under Standard Primitives subcategory, several text buttons appear that enable you to create some simple primitive objects. If you go ahead and click Sphere text button (not sphere icon at the top), several rollouts appear at the bottom of the Command Panel. These rollouts include Name and Color, Creation Method, Keyboard Entry, and Parameters. The rollouts for each primitive are slightly different, as well as the parameters within each rollout. You can ignore these rollouts and just create a sphere, simply click and drag within one of the viewports, and a sphere object appears.

Picture 3.3

If a Sphere button or any object button is selected, the color of it turns dark yellow to remind you that you are in creation mode. Clicking and dragging within any viewport creates an additional sphere. While in creation mode, you can create many spheres by clicking and dragging several times in one of the viewports. To get out of creation mode, right-click in the active viewport and click the Select Object button or one of the transform buttons on the main toolbar. After you select a button, several additional rollouts magically appear. These new rollouts hold the parameters for the selected object and are displayed in the Create panel below the Name and Color rollout. Altering these parameters changes the object. The button remains selected, allowing you to create more objects until you select a different button, click on a toolbar button, or right-click in the active viewport.

Give an object a name

You can give a name and color to every object in the scene as they are useful for locating and selecting objects. Each object is given a default name and random color when first created. The default name is the type of object followed by a number. For example, when you create a sphere object, Max labels it "Sphere01." These default names aren't very exciting and can be confusing if you have many objects. You can change the object's name at any time by modifying the Name field in the Name and Color rollout of the Command Panel.

In the Object Color dialog box shown in picture 3.4, if the Assign Random Colors option is selected, then a random color from the palette is chosen every time a new object is created. If this option is not selected, the color of all new objects is the same until you choose a different object color. You can select custom colors by clicking the Add Custom Colors button. This button opens a Color Selector dialog box. You can fill the entire row of Custom Colors by clicking repeatedly on the Add Color button. If you find a specific color that you like and want to use elsewhere, you can use the Color Clipboard utility to carry colors to other interfaces. You can access this utility using the Tools> Color Clipboard menu command, which opens the Utilities panel. Using this clipboard, you can open and save color configurations. The files are saved as Color Clipboard files with the .ccb extension.

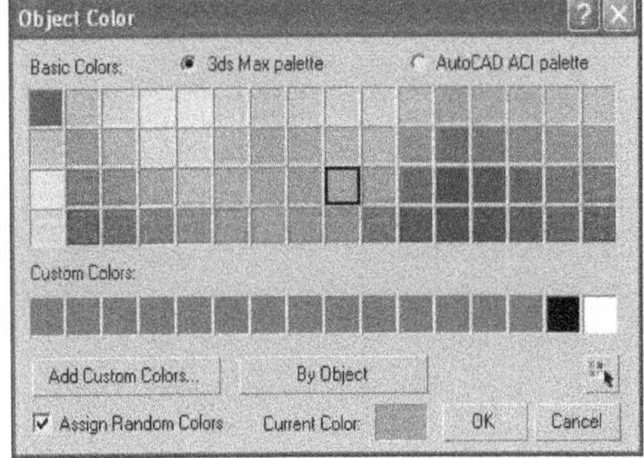

Picture 3.4

Creating objects

Primitive objects with a different number of dimensions require a different number of clicks and drags. For example, a sphere is one of the simplest objects to create. To create a sphere, click in a viewport to set the location of the sphere's center, drag the mouse to the desired radius, and release the mouse button to complete. A Box object, on the other hand, requires a click-and drag move to define the base (width and depth), and another drag-and-click move to set the height. If you ever get lost when defining these dimensions, check the Prompt Line to see what dimension the interface expects next. When you click a primitive object button, the Creation Method rollout appears and offers different methods for creating the primitives. For example, click the Sphere button, and the Creation Method rollout displays two options: Edge and Center. When you choose the Edge method, the first viewport click sets one edge of the sphere, and dragging and clicking again sets the diameter of the sphere. The default Center creation method defines the sphere's center location; dragging sets the sphere's radius. The creation method for each primitive can be different. For example, the Box primitive object has a creation method for creating perfect cubes. In the Create panel are actually two different subcategories of primitives: Standard Primitives and Extended Primitives. These primitives include a diverse range of objects like boxes and spheres, Cylinder, Torus, Teapot, Cone, GeoSphere, Tube, Pyramid, and Plane. You can create all these primitives from the Create panel. While dragging to create a primitive object and halfway through its creation you change your mind, you can right-click to eliminate the creation.

When creating a primitive object, you can define its location and dimensions by clicking in a viewport and dragging, or you can enter precise values in the Keyboard Entry rollout, located in the Create panel.

Within this rollout, you can enter the offset XYZ values for positioning the origin of the primitive and the dimensions of the object. The offset values are defined relative to the active construction plane that is usually the Home Grid. When all the dimension fields are set, click the Create button to create the actual primitive. You can create multiple objects by clicking the Create button several times. After a primitive is created, altering the fields in the Keyboard Entry rollout has no effect on the current object, but you can always use the Undo feature to try again.

There is one more rollout named Parameters rollout for all primitive objects. This rollout holds all the various settings for the object. Compared to the Keyboard Entry rollout, which you can use only when creating the primitive, you can use the Parameters rollout to alter the primitive's parameters before or after the creation of the object. For example, increasing the Radius value after creating an object makes an existing sphere larger. The parameters are different for each primitive object, but you can generally use them to control the dimensions, the number of segments that make up the object, and whether the object is sliced into sections. You can also select the Generate Mapping Coordinates option (which automatically creates material mapping coordinates that are used to position maps) and the Real-World Map Size option (which lets you define a texture's dimensions that are maintained regardless of the object size).

Understanding Segments value
Now we're going to create spheres and you'll see that changing Segments value will change the object's shape automatically. By the way spheres appear everywhere from sports balls to planets in space.
(1) Click on sphere text button in Command panel and make sure under Parameter rollout the Segment value is 32. Then drag the sphere in the viewport. The Segments value specifies the number of polygons that make up the sphere. The higher the number of segments, the smoother the sphere is. The default value of 32 produces a smooth sphere as the first sphere shown in picture 3.5.

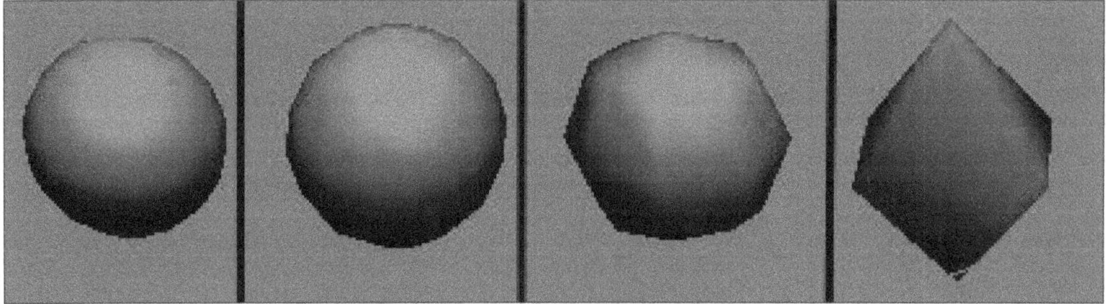

Picture 3.5
(2) You can go ahead and change the Segment value to 16, press enter and drag the sphere. It'll look similar to the second one shown in the picture. If you continue changing the Segment value to 8 and then 4, you'll have your spheres looking similar to 3rd and 4th spheres of this picture. A value of 4 produces a diamond-shaped object. The Smooth option lets you make the sphere smooth or faceted. Faceted spheres are useful for identifying faces for modifications.

Understanding Parameters for geometric shapes
Now we're using Hedra primitive objects to understand Parameters functions.
(1) In the Command panel Subcategory dropdown select Extended Primitives and click Hedra button.
(2) Click in the Top viewport, and drag to the left to create a simple Tetrahedron object. To adjust its settings, select the Tetra option in the Parameters rollout, set the P value in the Family Parameters

section to 1.0. Then enter a value of 50 for the Radius. Be sure to press the Enter key after entering a value to update the object. Enter the name **Tetrahedron** in the Object Name field.

(3) Click and drag again in the Top viewport to create another hedra object. In the Parameters rollout, select the Cube/Octa option, and enter a value of 1.0 in the Family Parameter's P field and a value of 50 in the Radius field. Name this object **Octagon**.

(4) Drag in the Top viewport to create another object. The Cube/Octa option is still selected. Enter a value of 1.0 in the Family Parameter's Q field this time, and set the Radius to 50. Name this object **Cube**.

(5) Drag in the Top viewport again to create the fourth hedra object. In the Parameters rollout, select the Dodec/Icos option, enter a value of 1.0 in the P field, and set the Radius value to 50. Name the object **Icosahedron**.

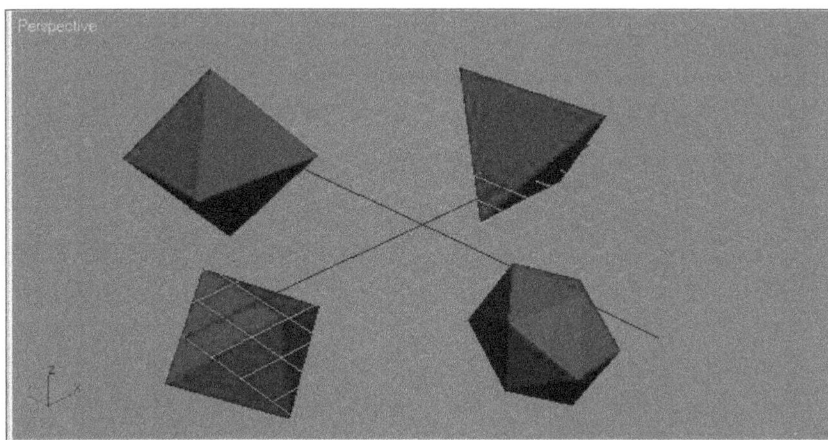

(6) Drag in the Top viewport to create the final object. With the Dodec/Icos option set, enter 1.0 for the Q value, and set the Radius to 50. Name this object **Dodecahedron**. After you're done, you'll have your viewport looking similar to the picture 3.6.

Picture 3.6

Using the Modify panel, you can return to these objects and change their parameters to learn the relationships between them. The relationship between P and Q can be described in this manner: When the P value is set to 1 and the Q value is set to 0, one shape of the pair is displayed. As the P value decreases, each vertex becomes a separate face. The edges of these new faces increase as the value is decreased down to 0. The same holds true for the Q value. Altering the P and Q parameters can create many unique shapes. For each Hedra, try the following combinations: P = 0, Q = 0; P = 1, Q = 0; P = 0, Q = 1; P = 0.5, Q = 0.5; P = 0.5, Q = 0; P = 0, Q = 0.5. These represent the main intermediate objects.

Lesson 14
Creating hemisphere

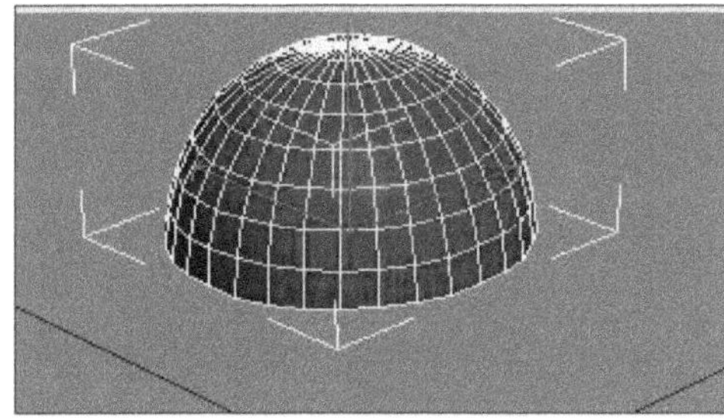

For creating a hemisphere, (1) Right-click on the word Perspective in Perspective viewport, select Configure and put enable Edged Faces under Rendering Method tab. (2) Select Sphere under Standard Primitives, in Parameters rollout enter the value 0.5 of Hemisphere, making sure the Segments value is already 32. When you draw, it should look like the picture 3.7. In the rollout, Slice option enables you to dissect the sphere into slices (like segmenting an orange).

Picture 3.7

For slicing up the sphere, enable Slice On button in rollout and in Slice From box enter 10 and in Slice To 250. Then draw it in the viewport. Change the Slice From and Slice To value to 80 and 250 and draw again, and one more time change them to 250 and 300 and draw in the viewport. Your scene should look similar to the picture 3.8. The Slice From and Slice To fields accept values ranging from 0 to 360 degrees. You can use the Slice feature on several primitives, including the sphere, cylinder, torus, cone, tube, oiltank, spindle, chamfercyl, and capsule.

Picture 3.8

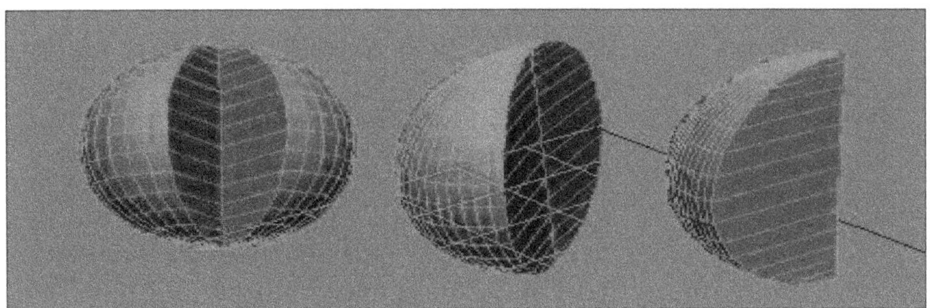

Like this, you can use a cylinder in many places—for example, as a pillar in front of a home or as a car driveshaft. To create one, first specify a base circle and then a height. The default number of sides is 18, which produces a smooth cylinder. Height and Cap Segments values define the number of polygons that make up the cylinder sides and caps. The Smooth and Slice options work the same as they do with a sphere (see the preceding section).

Modeling Torus and other objects

A **Torus** is a ring with a circular cross section. To create a Torus, you need to specify two radii values. The first is the value from the center of the Torus to the center of the ring; the second is the radius of the circular cross section. The default settings create a Torus with 24 segments and 12 sides. The Rotation and Twist options cause the sides to twist a specified value as the ring is circumnavigated. You can set the Segments values of 24, 12, and 6. And Twist values of 90 and 360. The higher the number of segments, the rounder the Torus looks when viewed from above. The default of 24 is sufficient to create a smooth Torus. The number of sides defines the circular smoothness of the cross section.

The Parameters rollout includes settings for four different Smooth options. The All option smoothes all edges, and the None option displays all polygons as faceted. The Sides option smoothes edges between sides, resulting in a Torus with banded sides. The Segment option smoothes between segment edges, resulting in separate smooth sections around the Torus. The Slice options work with a Torus the same way as they do with the sphere and cylinder objects.

The **teapot** is another object that, like the sphere, is easy to create. Within the Parameters rollout, you can specify the number of Segments, whether the surface is smooth or faceted, and which parts to display, including Body, Handle, Spout, and Lid. You may recognize most of these primitives as standard shapes, with the exception of the teapot. The teapot has a special place in computer graphics. In early computer graphics development labs, the teapot was chosen as the test model for many early algorithms. It is still included as a valuable benchmark for computer graphics programmers.

The **Cone** object, whether used to create ice cream cones or megaphones, is created exactly like the cylinder object except that the second cap can have a radius different from that of the first. You create it by clicking and dragging to specify the base circle, dragging to specify the cone's height, and then dragging again for the second cap to create a Cone. In addition to the two cap radii and the Height, parameter options include the number of Height and Cap Segments, the number of Sides, and the Smooth and Slice options.

The **Tube** primitive is useful any time you need a pipe object. You can also use it to create ring-shaped objects that have rectangular cross sections. Creating a Tube object is verysimilar to the Cylinder and Cone objects. Tube parameters include two radii for the inner and outer tube walls. Tubes also have the Smooth and Slice options.

A **ChamferBox** primitive is a box with smoothed edges. The parameter that determines the amount of roundness applied to an edge is Fillet. In many ways, this object is just a simple extension of the Box primitive. The only additions in the Parameters rollout are two fields for controlling the Fillet dimension and the Fillet Segments. You can use the Fillet values of 0, 5, 10, 20, and 30 and the Smooth option turned on.

The next object you should know about is **RingWave**. It is used to create a simple gear or a sparkling sun. It has both Inner and Outer Edge Breakup settings. You'll see the edges change over the different frames. It consists of two circles that make up a ring. You can set the circle edges to be wavy and even fluctuate over time. You can also use RingWaves to simulate rapidly expanding gases that would result from a planetary explosion. You can get the idea of it from the picture 3.9 shown below.

If you're considering a Shockwave effect, then you should look into using a RingWave primitive. The Radius setting and the inner edge define the outer edge by the Ring Width. This ring can also have a Height. The Radial and Height Segments and the number of Sides determine the complexity of the object. The RingWave Timing controls set the expansion values. The Start Time is the frame where the ring begins at zero, the Grow Time is the number of frames required to reach its full size, and the End Time is the frame where the RingWave object stops expanding. The No Growth option prevents the object from expanding, and it remains the same size from the Start frame to the End frame. The Grow and Stay option causes the RingWave to expand from the Start Time until the Grow Time frame is reached, and then remain full grown until the End Time. The Cyclic Growth begins expanding the objects until the Grow Time is reached. It then starts again from zero and expands repeatedly until the End Time is reached. The last two sections of the Parameters rollout define how the inner and outer edges look and are animated. If the Edge Breakup option is on, then the rest of the settings are enabled. These additional settings control the number of Major and Minor Cycles, the Width Flux for these cycles, and the Crawl Time, which is the number of frames to animate. The Surface Parameters section includes an option for creating Texture Coordinates, which are the same as mapping coordinates for applying textures. There is also an option to Smooth the surface of the object.

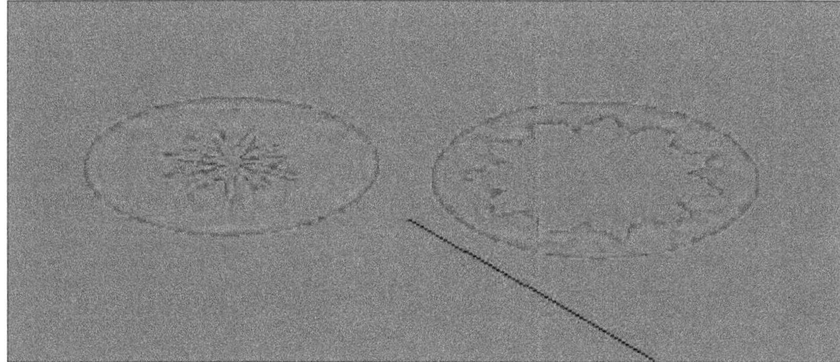

Picture 3.9

Creating a pie using RingWave

Although the RingWave object can be animated, you also can use it to create static objects such as this pie, or moving objects such as a set of gears. This book has several lessons dedicated to animation and animating things is quite easy in Max. I really thank Max for this. But this time, it is advisable that you can concentrate more and more on modeling and designing.

(1) Go to Extended Primitives> RingWave, and drag in the Top viewport to create a RingWave object. You see the picture 4.0 for help.

(2) In the Parameters rollout, set the Radius to 115, the Ring Width to 90, and the Height to 30. Make sure that you enter the value correctly and press enter after each entry.

(3) In the RingWave Timing section, select the No Growth option. Then enable the Outer Edge Breakup option, set the Major Cycles to 25, the Width Flux to 4.0, and the Minor Cycles to 0.

Picture 4.0

(4) Enable the Inner Edge Breakup option. Set the Major Cycles to 6, the Width Flux to 15, and the Minor Cycles to 25 with a Width Flux of 10.Though it is done, but if you want, you can add Taper modifier to it by selecting Modifiers> Parametric Deformers> Taper to apply the Taper modifier and set the Amount to 0.1.

To see the glimpse of animation, when the pie is created, you can press AutoKey N on your keyboard. This will activate animation mode and you will see the Time Frame (a bar) at the very bottom of Max screen turned red. You can drag the Time Slider to number 100, then move or rotate the pie a little and press N key again to exit animation mode. Select Animation in the Menu bar at the top> Make Animation> Create and you'll see the pie moving. It's cool, isn't it?

Creating Torus Knots

A Torus Knot has circular cross section that follows a 3D curve. The Parameters rollout lets you specify the base curve to be a circle instead of a knot. A knot is a standard, mathematically defined 3D curve. Below the Radius and Segment parameters are the P and Q values. These values can be used to create different kinds of knots. The P value is a mathematical factor for computing how the knot winds about its vertical axis. The maximum value is 25, which makes the knot resemble a tightly wound spool. The Q value causes the knot to wind horizontally. It also has a maximum value of 25. If you set both values to the same number, it'll results in a simple circular ring.

The A section of the picture 4.1 shows some of the beautiful shapes created by altering the P and Q values of a Torus Knot. These Torus Knots have these values: the first has P = 3, Q = 2; the second has P = 1, Q = 3; the third has P = 10, Q = 15; the fourth has P = 15, Q = 20; and the fifth has P = 25, Q = 25.

The section B shows the shapes in which the Base Curve is set to Circle, and the P and Q values become disabled, and the Warp Count and Warp Height fields become active. These fields control the number of ripples in the ring and their height. Picture 4.1 shown below displays several possibilities. From left to right, the settings are Warp Count = 5, Warp Height = 0.5; Warp Count = 10, Warp Height = 0.5; Warp Count = 20, Warp Height = 0.5; Warp Count = 50, Warp Height = 0.5; and Warp Count = 100, Warp Height = 0.75.

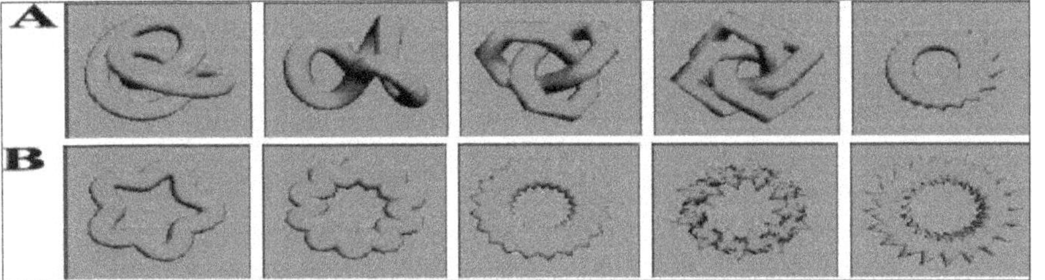

Picture 4.1

In addition to the Base Curve settings, you can also control several settings for the Cross Section. The Radius and Sides values determine the size of the circular cross section and the number of segments used to create the cross section. The Eccentricity value makes the circular cross section elliptical by stretching it along one of its axes. The Twist value rotates each successive cross section relative to the previous one creating a twisting look along the object. The Lumps value sets the number of lumps that appear in the Torus Knot, and the Lump Height and Offset values set the height and starting point of these lumps. The Smooth options work just like for the Torus object by smoothing the entire object, just the sides, or none. You can set the U and V axis Offset and Tiling values for the mapping coordinates.

Lesson 15
Creating a bendable straw
Now this lesson with the tutorial will prove by itself how simple it is. Before writing the steps of this tutorial I referred to the other books but I found everywhere the same shallow efforts made by the authors telling to download half-made stuff from somewhere and remaining half to do. This would be quite frustrating to the learner like you, as it was for me. So the steps written in this book, and only in this book, help you start from SCRATCH and I believe you get the ability to create everything on you own. Some authors make the learning of Max more complicated so that the publisher can sell more stuff along with the book. Hope you understand their marketing tricks. But here you will find everything clean and sacred.

(1) Go to Standard Primitives> select Tube> pick up a color (preferably brown) and drag in Perspective viewport. It'll take three mouse clicks.
(2) Select it with Select tool, click Modify tab in Command panel, and in Parameter rollout set Radius 1 value to 9, Radius 2 value to 11, and Height to 40.
(3) With the object selected, click on Move tool at the top and go to the status bar at the bottom in the middle of Max screen to set the object's location. Now enter X value to 2.5, Y to 40, and Z to 22. Keep pressing Enter key after every entry. Don't worry; everything is error-proof because I do the same before I write in the book.

(4) Click Create tab in Command panel> Standard Primitives> Tube> pick up the same color and drag in the viewport again. Set Radius 1, Radius 2 and Height value same as above. But for location, enter X value to 2.5, Y to 25 and Z to -25 (minus).

(5) While second tube is selected, click on rotate tool at the top and in left viewport rotate the same (second tube) all the way upside down. With Move tool, push the second tube up where it was.

(6) Go to Extended Primitives> Hose> Pick up light blue color and Parameters rollout enable Bound to Object Pivots.

(7) Now drag a Hose in the middle where the two straws (tubes) meet. In Parameters rollout, click on the Pick Top Object button, and select the top Tube object. Then click on the Pick Bottom Object button, and select the bottom Tube object. This step positions the Hose object between the two Tube pieces.

(8) In the Hose Parameters rollout, set the Tension for both Tubes to 10.0. Set the Segments to 40, the Starts value to 0, the Ends value to 100, the Cycles to 10, and the Diameter to 40. Make sure that the Renderable option is enabled, and enable the Round Hose option with a Diameter of 15.0. That's it. Picture 4.2 shows the DWF view of this scene.

Picture 4.2

The Hose is a flexible connector to be positioned between two other objects. It acts much like a spring. In the Hose Parameters rollout, it can be specified as a Free Hose or Bound to Object Pivots. If the Bound to Object Pivots option is selected, then two Pick Object buttons appear for the Top and Bottom objects. Once bound to two objects, the hose stretches between the two objects when either is moved. You can also set the Tension for each bound object. For either the Bound Hose or Free Hose, you can set the number of Segments that make up the hose; whether the flexible section is enabled; to smooth along the Sides, Segments, neither, or all; whether the hose is Renderable; and to Generate Mapping Coordinates for applying texture maps. If the flexible section is enabled, then you can set where the flexible section Starts and Ends, the number of Cycles, and its Diameter. You can also set the Hose Shape to Round, Rectangular, or D-Section.

Working with object parameters

Primitive objects provide a good starting point for many of the other modeling types. They also provide a good way to show off parameter-based modeling. All objects have parameters. These parameters help define how the object looks. For example, consider the primitive objects. The primitive objects contained in Max are parametric. Parametric objects are mathematically defined, and you can change them by modifying their parameters. The easiest object modifications to make are simply changing these parameters. For example, a sphere with a radius of 4 can be made into a sphere with a radius of 10 by simply typing a 10 in the Radius field. The viewports display these changes automatically when you press the Enter key. When an object is first created, its parameters are displayed in the Parameters rollout of the Create panel. As long as the object remains the current object, you can modify its parameters using this rollout. After you select a different tool or object, the Parameters rollout is no longer accessible from the Create panel. It can be found from then on under the Modify panel.

A box of gems

In this tutorial, you're going to create a box, and then you'll fill it with a number of Hedra primitives and alter the object properties in the Modify panel to create a diverse offering of gems.

(1) Select Awning from Subcategory of Command panel and draw it in the viewport. In Parameters rollout set Height to 20, Width to 40 and Depth to 25. And use Rotate tool to place the box in right position.

(2) Go to Extended Primitives> Hedra and create several Hedra objects. The size of the objects doesn't matter at this time. You can see the picture 4.3 for help.

(3) Open the Modify panel, and select one of the Hedra objects. Alter the values in the Parameters rollout to produce a nice gem. Repeat this step for all Hedra objects.

Picture 4.3

Getting skilled with Max helps you to work with AutoCAD program also which is used is used by a vast number of engineers and architects to design the layouts for building physical structures. You can find many of the architectural objects in the subcategory of AEC Objects. The Foliage category includes several different plants all listed in the Favorite Plants rollout. At the bottom of the Favorite Plants rollout is a button called Plant Library that opens a dialog box where you can see the details of all the plants, including the total number of faces. The winner is the Banyan tree with 100,000 faces. Using the Parameters rollout, you can set the Height, Density, and Pruning values for each of these plants. Also, depending on the tree type, you can select to show the Leaves, Trunk, Fruit, Branches, Flowers, and Roots, and you can set the Level of Detail to Low, Medium, or High.

Lesson 16
Selecting objects

In a complex scene of many objects, lights, cameras, shapes, and so on, selecting the exact object that you want can be difficult. Though one simple way is that if you continue to click an object that is already selected, then the object directly behind the object you clicked on is selected. For example, if you have a row of spheres lined up, you can select the third sphere by clicking three times on the first object. By the way in complicated scenes, finding an object is often much easier if it has a relevant name. So be sure to name your new objects using the Name and Color rollout.

Choosing Edit> Select by> Name opens the Select Objects dialog box. Clicking the Select by Name button on the main toolbar, positioned to the right of the Select Object button, or pressing the Keyboard shortcut, H, can also open this dialog box. It displays all objects in the current scene by name. You select objects by clicking their names in the list and then clicking the Select button. To pick and choose several objects, hold down the Ctrl key while selecting. Holding down the Shift key selects a range of objects. You can also type an object name in the field above the name list. All objects that match the typed characters are selected. The Sort options affect how the list is displayed. Selecting the Sort by Size option sorts the objects by the number of faces, and this is an easy way to find the most complicated object in the scene. By the way pressing the Q keyboard shortcut selects the Select Object mode in the main toolbar.

If you need to modify or transform several objects at once, you can select multiple objects in several ways. With the Select by Name dialog box open, you can choose several objects from the list using the standard Ctrl and Shift keys. Holding down the Ctrl key selects or deselects multiple list items, but holding down the Shift key selects all consecutive list items between the first selected and the second selected items. The Ctrl key also works when selecting objects in the viewport using one of the main toolbar Select buttons. You can tell whether you're in select mode by looking for a button that's highlighted yellow. If you hold down the Ctrl key and click an object, then the object is added to the current selection set. If you click an item that is already selected, then it is deselected. If you drag over multiple objects while holding down the Ctrl key, then all items in the dragged selection are added to the current selection set. The Alt key deselects objects from the current selection set, which is opposite of what the Ctrl key does.

When you finally select the exact objects that you want to work with, you can disable any other selections using the Selection Lock toggle button on the Status Bar which looks like a lock. When this button is enabled, it is colored yellow, and clicking objects in the viewports won't have any effect on the current selection. The keyboard shortcut toggle for this command is the spacebar. One more thing that you should know about the selection is Named Selection Set. When you have a group of selected objects, you can establish a selection set. Once established as a selection set, you can recall this group of selected objects at any time by selecting its name from the Named Selection Set drop-down list on the main toolbar, or by opening the Named Selection Sets dialog box. You can access this dialog box using the Edit Named Selection Sets button on the main toolbar or by selecting the Edit> Named Selection Sets menu command. To establish a selection set, type a name in the Named Selection Set drop-down list toward the right end of the main toolbar or use the dialog box. You can also isolate the current selection by going to Tools> Isolate Selection (Alt+Q). This command hides all objects except for the selected object.

Freezing objects

If you have an object in a correct position, you can freeze it to prevent it from being moved accidentally or you can hide it from the viewports completely. A key difference between these modes is that frozen objects are still rendered, but hidden objects are not. You can hide or freeze objects in a scene by selecting the Hide or Freeze options in the Object Properties dialog box. You can also hide and freeze objects using the Display Floater dialog box, which you access by choosing Tools> Display Floater. The Hide option makes the selected object in the scene invisible, and the Freeze option turns the selected object dark gray and doesn't allow it to be transformed or selected. You cannot select hidden objects by clicking in the viewport.

Working with Layers

Here is what draws your attention again. As you know, layers provide a way to separate scene objects into easy-to-select and easy-to-work-with groupings. These individual layers have properties that can

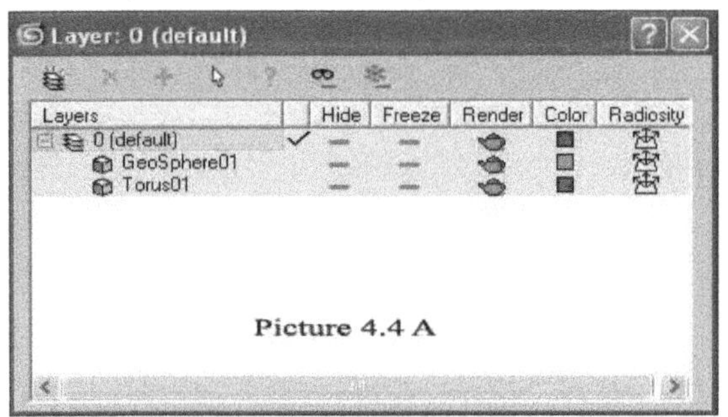

Picture 4.4 A

then be turned on and off. You create, access, and manage layers through the Layer Manager Dialog box, and this dialog box is a floater that can remain open as you work with objects in the viewports. You can access the Layer Manager using the Tools> Layer Manager, or by clicking the Layer Manager Button on the main toolbar. The Layer Manager lists all the layers and the objects contained within each layer. The picture 4.4 A shows a layer with two objects in it.

The Layer Manger dialog box has some buttons at the top just below the blue border. The first one: Create New Layer - creates a new layer that includes the selected objects, the second: Delete Highlighted Empty Layers - deletes a layer if the layer is highlighted and empty, third: Add Selected Objects to Highlighted Layer Adds any selected objects to the current highlighted layer, fourth: Select Highlighted Objects and Layers - selects in the viewports any highlighted layers or objects, fifth: Highlight Selected Object's Layers - highlights the layer of the viewport's selected object in the Layer Manager, sixth: Hide/Unhide All Layers - toggles between hiding and un-hiding all layers, and seventh: Freeze/Unfreeze All Layers - toggles between freezing and unfreezing all layers.

After you've set up your layers, you can control them using the Layers toolbar rather than having the Layer Manager open. You can access the Layers toolbar (shown in picture 4.4 B) by right-clicking the main toolbar away from the buttons and selecting the Layers toolbar from the popup menu or by selecting the Customize> Show UI> Floating Toolbars menu command. As you see six buttons in it, 1st is Layer Manager Button, 2nd is Layer Selection dropdown list, 3rd is Create New Layer, 4th is Add Selection

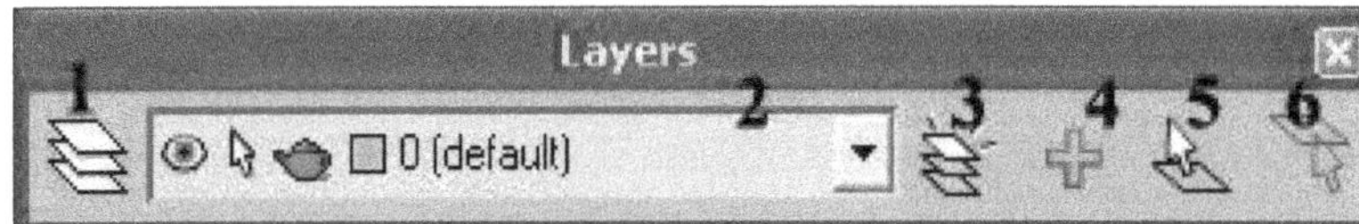

to Current Layer, 5th is Select Objects in Current Layer, and 6th is Set Current Layer to Selection's Layer.

Picture 4.4 B

With the Layer Manager open, you can create new layers by clicking the Create New Layer button. This adds a new layer to the manager, names it "Layer01," and includes any selected objects as part of the layer. If you click the layer's name, you can rename it. Layer 0 is the default layer to which all objects are added, if other layers don't exist. Layer 0 cannot be renamed.

Using the Layer List

The main section of the Layer Manager (and repeated in the Layers toolbar) is the layer list and its columns, which allow you to turn certain properties on and off. The properties in the columns include Hide, Freeze, Render, Color, and Radiosity. If a property is enabled, a simple icon is displayed; if disabled, a dash is displayed. If an object is set to get its property from the layer (by clicking the ByLayer button in the Object Properties dialog box), a dot icon is displayed. Individual objects within a layer can have different properties. You can sort the column properties by clicking on the column head. The Layer Manager also includes a right-click pop-up menu that includes many of the same commands found as buttons, but a unique set of commands found in the right-click pop-up menu are the Cut and Paste commands. With these commands, you can select objects in one layer to cut and paste into another layer. If you forget to select the correct layer for the new objects, you can select the objects in the viewports, highlight the correct layer, and use the Add Selected Objects to Highlighted Layer button to add the objects to the correct layer.

Lesson 17
Working with the Transform Gizmos
The three buttons - Select and Move, Select and Rotate, and Select and Uniform Scale are called transform buttons. When you select an object in the viewport and click any of these transform buttons, the Transform Gizmos appear at the center (pivot point) of the selected object. The type of gizmo that appears depends on the transformation mode that is selected. You can choose from three different gizmos, one for each transformation type. Each gizmo includes three color-coded arrows, circles, and lines representing the X-, Y-, and Z-axes. The X-axis is colored red, the Y-axis is colored green, and the Z-axis is colored blue. If the Transform Gizmo is not visible, you can enable it by choosing Views> Show Transform Gizmo or by pressing the X key to toggle it on and off. You can use the – (minus) and = (equal) keys to decrease or increase the gizmo's size. The Gizmos panel in the Preference Settings dialog box lets you control how the Transform Gizmos look.

Using the Align Commands
The Align commands are an easy way to automatically transform objects. You can use these commands to line up object centers or edges, align normals and highlights, align to views and grids, and even line up cameras. Any object that you can transform, you can align, including lights, cameras, and Space Warps. After selecting the object to be aligned, click the Align flyout button on the main toolbar or choose Tools> Align (or press Alt+A). The cursor changes to the Align icon. Now, click a target object with which you want to align all the selected objects. Clicking the target object opens the Align Selection dialog box with the target object's name displayed in the dialog box's title. This dialog box can align objects along any axes by their Minimum, Center, Pivot, or Maximum points. The Align Selection dialog box includes settings for the X, Y, and Z positions to line up the Minimum, Center, Pivot Point, or Maximum dimensions for the selected or target object's bounding box. As you change the settings in the dialog box, the objects reposition themselves, but at the end you have to click Apply or OK button.

Using Grids
The Home Grid is to give you a reference point for creating objects in 3D space. At the center of each grid are two darker lines. These lines meet at the origin point for the World Coordinate System where the coordinates for X, Y, and Z are all 0.0. This point is where all objects are placed by default. In addition to the Home Grid, you can create and place new grids in the scene. These grids are not rendered, but you can use them to help you locate and align objects in 3D space.

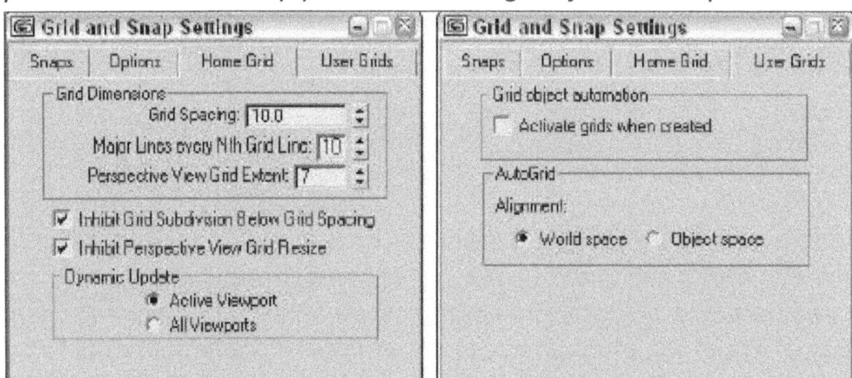

You can turn the Home Grid on and off by choosing Views> Grid> Show Home Grid or using G key in selected viewport. If the Home Grid is the only grid in the scene, then by default it is also the construction grid where new objects are positioned when created. Picture 4.5

You can access the Home Grid parameters (shown in picture 4.5) by choosing Customize> Grid and Snap Settings. You can also access this dialog box by right-clicking the Snap, Angle Snap, or Percent Snap toggle buttons located on the main toolbar. In the Home Grid panel of the Grid and Snap Settings dialog box, you can set how often Major Lines appear, as well as Grid Spacing. (The Spacing value for the active grid is displayed on the status bar.) You can also specify to dynamically update the grid view in all viewports or just in the active one.

Using Snap Options
If you try to line up the exact positions of an object by hand, it appears to be extremely frustrating. But using the Snap feature sets everything all right. With the Snap feature enabled, an object automatically moves (or snaps) to the specified snap position when you place it close enough. If you enable the Snap features, they affect any transformations that you make in a scene. Snap points are defined in the Grid and Snap Settings dialog box that you can open by choosing Customize> Grid and Snap Settings or by right-clicking any of the first three Snap buttons on the main toolbar. These Snap buttons have a small magnet icon in them. The Snaps panel includes many different points to snap to depending on the object type. With the Snaps feature enabled, the cursor becomes blue crosshairs wherever a snap point is located. You have several snap options in the main toolbar.

Cloning Objects
Cloning objects is the process of creating copies of objects. These copies can maintain an internal connection (called an instance or a reference) to the original object that allows them to be modified along with the original object. For example, if you create a school desk from a Box primitive and modify its parameters, the same resulting effect is applied to all instances of the original. One method is to use the Edit> Clone (Ctrl+V) menu command. And another method is to transform an object while holding down the Shift key. When a clone is created with the Clone menu, it is positioned directly on top of the original, which makes distinguishing it from the original difficult. To verify that a clone has been created, open the Select by Name dialog box by pressing H and look for the cloned object (it has the same name, but an incremented number has been added). To see both objects, click the Select and Move button on the main toolbar and move one of the objects away from the other. But an easier way to create clones is always Shift key with any of the transformation tool.

Mirroring Objects
When an object is selected, the Mirror command creates a clone (or No Clone if you so choose). To open the Mirror dialog box, choose Tools> Mirror, or click the Mirror button located on the main toolbar. Within the Mirror dialog box, you can specify an axis or plane about which to mirror the selected object. You can also define an offset value. As with the other clone commands, you can specify whether the clone is to be a Copy, an Instance, or a Reference, or you can choose No Clone, which flips the object around the axis you specify.

Using the Snapshot command
Though you'll learn in detail about Snapshot command when you'll start learning animation in Max, here are a few interesting things about it. The Snapshot command creates copies, instances, references, or even meshes of a selected object as it follows an animation path. For example, you could create a series of footprints that magically appear by positioning the first footprint at frame 1 and the last footprint at frame 100, and then choose Tools> Snapshot and enter the number of steps to appear between these two in the Snapshot dialog box. As the animation plays, new footprints will appear along the animation path at regular intervals. Be aware that the Snapshot command works only with objects that have an animation path defined.

Creating a tower of cubes

To create a tower of cubes with the Snapshot tool, follow these steps:

(1) Click on the Box button in the Create panel, select the Cube option in the Creation Method rollout, and drag in the Top viewport. In the Parameters rollout, set the cube's height, weight and length to 30.

(2) Select Create> Shapes> Helix, and click and drag in the Top viewport three times to create a helix

spline. Set its Radius 1 value to 115, its Radius 2 to 0, its Height to 125, and the number of Turns to 5.

(3) Select the cube object, open the Motion panel in the Command Panel, and click the Trajectories button. Set the Start Time to 0, the End Time to 100, and the Samples to 100. Then click the Convert From button, and select the helix spline in the viewports. This animates the cube along the helix spline (shown in picture 4.6).

(4) Select Tools> Snapshot to open the Snapshot dialog box. Select the Range option, set the number of Copies to 100, and select the Instance option. Then click the OK button.

Picture 4.6

Using the Spacing tool

If you don't have an animated path where you want clone objects, then Snapshot tools won't help. In that case the Spacing tool can position clones at regular intervals along a path by either selecting a path and the number of cloned objects or by picking two points in the viewport. You access the Spacing tool by clicking the last button in the flyout under the Array button on the Extras toolbar (the Extras toolbar can be made visible by right-clicking on the main toolbar away from the buttons). You can also access it using the Tools> Spacing Tool (Shift+I) menu command. At the top of this dialog box are two buttons: Pick Path and Pick Points. If a path is selected, its name appears on the Pick Path button. You can also specify Count, Spacing, Start Offset, and End Offset values. The drop-down list offers several preset options, including Divide Evenly, Free Center, End Offset, and more. These values and preset options are used to define the number and spacing of the objects. The spacing and position of the objects depend on the values that are included. For example, if you include only a Count value, then the objects are evenly spaced along the path including an object at each end. If an offset value is included, then the first or last item is moved away from the end by the offset value. If a Spacing value is included, then the number of objects required to meet this value is included automatically.

Lesson 18

Grouping and Linking Objects

When a scene becomes more complex, you need to group objects together. Max's grouping features enable you to organize all the objects that you're dealing with, thereby making your workflow more efficient. Another way of organizing objects is to build a linked hierarchy. A linked hierarchy attaches, or links, one object to another and makes it possible to transform the attached object by moving the one to which it is linked. The arm is a classic example of a linked hierarchy—when the shoulder rotates, so do the elbow, wrist, and fingers. Establishing linked hierarchies can make moving, positioning, and animating many objects easy. The Group menu commands let you control how objects are grouped together. Selecting several objects and using the Group command (choose Group> Group) opens a simple dialog box where you can type a name for the group. You can always identify groups in the Select by Name dialog box because they are surrounded by square brackets, and groups appear in bold in the Name and Color rollout of the Command Panel. The Ungroup command (select the desired group and choose Group> Ungroup) disassembles the group and is active only if a group is selected. You can nest groups one inside another. You can also open and close groups, which means that you can attach or detach objects from the group or move individual group objects within the group. The Explode command un-groups all nested group objects.

At the bottom of the Group menu is a menu item called Assembly. The difference between a group and an assembly is that an assembly can include a light object with a Luminaire helper object as its head. This enables you to build light fixtures where the light is actually grouped (or assembled) with the light stand objects. Once built, you can control the light by selecting and moving the light assembly.

Parent, Child, and Root Relationships
All objects in a scene, whether linked or not, belong to a hierarchy. A parent object is an object that controls any secondary, or child, objects linked to it. A child object is an object that is linked to and controlled by a parent. A parent object can have many children, but a child can have only one parent. Additionally, an object can be both a parent and a child at the same time. A hierarchy is the complete set of linked objects that includes these types of relationships. Each hierarchy can have several branches or sub-trees. Any parent with two or more children represents the start of a new branch.

The objects that aren't linked to any other objects are, by default, children of the world object, which is an imaginary object that holds all objects. To establish hierarchies you can use the Link and Unlink buttons found on the main toolbar. The main toolbar includes two buttons that you can use to build a hierarchy: Link and Unlink. The order of selection defines which object becomes the parent and which becomes the child. To link two objects, click the Link button. When you're in Link mode, the Link button is highlighted dark yellow. With the Link button highlighted, click an object, which will be the child, and drag a line to the target parent object. The cursor arrow changes to the link icon when it is over a potential parent. When you release the mouse button, the parent object flashes once and the link is established. If you drag the same child object to a different parent, the link to the previous parent is replaced by the link to the new parent. Once linked, all transformations applied to the parent are applied equally to its children about the parent's pivot point. A pivot point is the center about which the object rotates.

Unlinking objects
The Unlink button is used to destroy links, but only to the parent. For example, if a selected object has both children and a parent, clicking the Unlink button destroys the link to the parent of the selected object, but not the links to its children. To eliminate all links for an entire hierarchy, double-click an object to select its entire hierarchy and click the Unlink button. The Display panel includes a rollout that lets you display all the links in the viewports.
After links have been established, you can see linked objects listed as a hierarchy in several places. The Select Objects dialog box, opened with the Select by Name button (or with the H key), can display objects in this manner, as well as the Schematic and Track Views. You can choose to see the links between the selected objects in the viewports by selecting the Display Links option in the Link Display rollout of the Display panel. The Display Links option shows links as lines that run between the pivot points of the objects with a diamond-shaped marker at the end of each line; these lines and markers are the same color as the object.

Using the Schematic View Window

A great way to organize and select objects is by using the Schematic View window because of its ability to link objects. In normal viewports, linking objects is tricky as some objects are small and hidden behind other items, but in the Schematic View you can do it easily with its nodes that are all of the same size. Every object in the Schematic View is displayed as a rectangular box. These boxes, or nodes, are connected to show the relationships among them. You can rearrange them and save the customized views for later access. You access the Schematic View window via the Graph Editors menu command or by clicking its button on the main toolbar. When the window opens, it floats on top of the Max interface and can be moved by dragging its title bar. You can also resize the window by dragging on its borders. The window is modeless and lets you access the viewports and buttons in the interface beneath it.

Applying modifiers

An object can have several modifiers applied to it. Modifiers can be applied using the Modifiers menu or by selecting the modifier from the Modifier List drop-down list located at the top of the Modify panel directly under the object name. Selecting a modifier in the Modifiers menu or from the Modifier List applies the modifier to the current selected object. Modifiers can be applied to multiple objects if several objects are selected (Ctrl+click). Some modifiers aren't available for some types of objects. For example, the Extrude and Lathe modifiers are enabled only when a spline shape is selected.

After a modifier is applied, its parameters appear in rollouts within the Command Panel. The Modifier Stack rollout, shown in picture 4.7, lists the base object and all the modifiers that have been applied to an object. Any new modifiers applied to an object are placed at the top of the stack. By selecting a modifier from the list in the Modifier Stack, all the parameters for that specific modifier are displayed in rollouts. You can increase or decrease the size of the Modifier Stack by dragging the horizontal bar that appears beneath the Modifier Stack buttons. Beneath the Modifier Stack are five buttons (shown in picture 4.7 below] line drawn) that affect the selected modifier. (1) Pin Stack – it makes the parameters for the selected modifier available for editing even if another object is selected. (2) Show End Result On/Off Toggle – it shows the end results of all the modifiers in the entire Stack when enabled and only the modifiers up to the current selected modifier if disabled. (3) Make Unique – it is used to break any instance or reference links to the selected object. After you click this button, an object will no longer be modified along with the other objects for which it was an instance or reference. It works for Base Object and modifiers. (4) Remove Modifier from the Stack – it is used to delete a modifier from the Stack or unbind a Space Warp if one is selected. Deleting a modifier restores it to the same state it was in before the modifier was applied. (5) Configure Modifier Sets – it opens a pop-up menu where you can select to show a set of modifiers as buttons above the Modifier Stack. You can also select which modifier set appears at the top of the list of modifiers. The pop-up menu also includes an option to configure and define the various sets of modifiers.

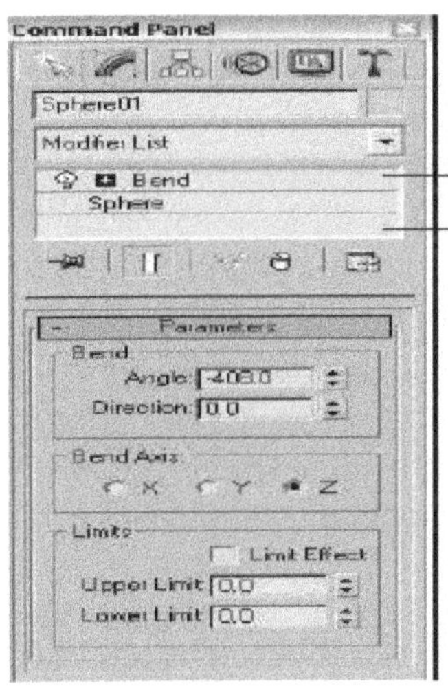

Picture 4.7

If you right-click on a modifier, a pop-up menu appears which includes commands to rename, delete, Cut, Copy, Paste, and Paste the selected modifier. The Cut command deletes the modifier from the current object but makes it available for pasting onto other objects. The Copy command retains the modifier for the current object and makes it available to paste onto another object. You can also apply modifiers for the current object onto other objects by dragging the modifier from the Modifier Stack and dropping it on the other object in a viewport. If you look closely at the Modifier Stack, you will notice that it includes some visual clues that help you identify instances and references. Regular object and modifier copies appear in normal text, but instances appear in bold. This applies to both objects and modifiers. If a modifier is applied to two or more objects, then it appears in italic.

Creating a molecular chain

(1) Go to Standard Primitives> Plane, and drag in the Top viewport to create a Plane object. Set its Length to **300**, its Width to **60**, its Length Segments to **11**, and its Width Segments to **1**.

(2) With the Plane object selected, select Modifiers> Parametric Deformers> Lattice to apply the Lattice

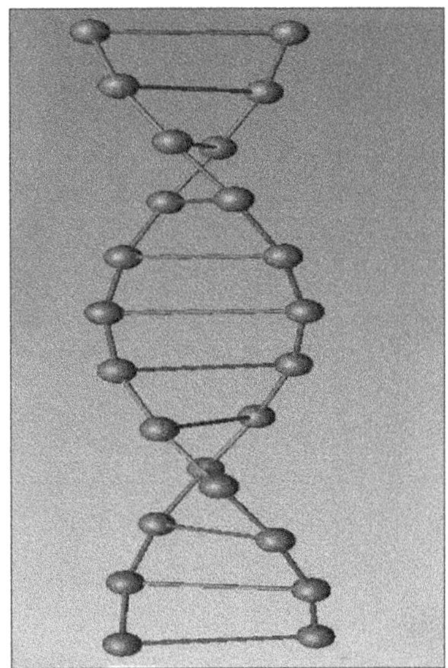

modifier. Enable the Apply to Entire Object option. Then set the Struts Radius value to **1.0** with **12** sides and the Joints Base Type to **Icosa** with a Radius of **6.0** and a Segments value of **6**.

(3) Select Modifiers> Parametric Deformers> Twist, and set the Twist Angle to **360** about the Y-axis.

(4) Notice that the Sphere objects have been twisted along with the Plane object. You can fix this by switching the modifier order in the Modifier Stack. Select the Lattice modifier, and **drag and drop** it above the Twist modifier in the stack. This step corrects the elongated spheres (see picture 4.8). Changing the order of the modifiers in the Stack can affect the end result.

Covering all the modifiers in a single lesson will not be possible, so you'll learn about some other modifiers in the following lessons. When you click the Modifier tab at the top of Max screen, you see all the various modifiers organized in several distinct sets which bring magnificent effects to the objects drawn in the viewport.

Picture 4.8

One important feature that you would love to know here in Max is setting a stopping point for the current scene. The Hold command saves the scene into a temporary buffer for easy recovery. After a scene is set with the Hold command (Alt+Ctrl+H), you can bring it back instantly with the Fetch command (Alt+Ctrl+F). These commands provide a quick way to backtrack on modifications to a scene or project without your having to save and reload the project.

Bend modifier

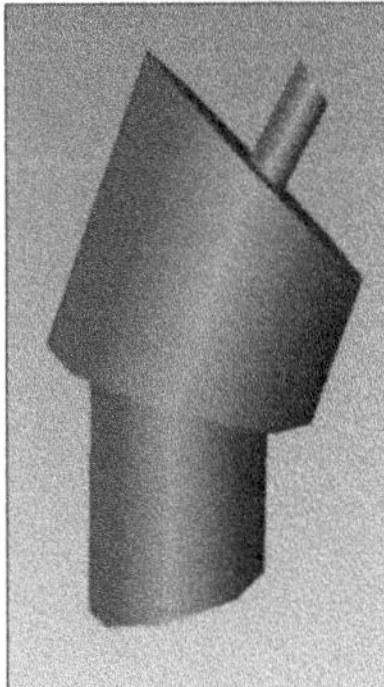

The Bend modifier can bend an object along any axis. Bend parameters include the Bend Angle and Direction, Bend Axis, and Limits. To bend a tree using the Bend modifier, follow these steps:

(1) Go to Dynamic Objects in Command panel> Damper and draw in the viewport.

(2) In Parameter rollout set Base Diameter to 40, Height to 35, Main Diameter to 60, and Height to 40.

(3) With the damper selected, select the Modifiers> Parametric Deformers> Bend menu command.

(4) In the Parameters rollout found in the Modify panel, set the Bend Axis to Z and the Bend Angle to 60. The damper bends as desired (shown in picture 4.9).

Picture 4.9

Taper modifier

Now let's see some more modifiers applicable to this damper. First to make this damper straight, select it, click Modifier tab in Command panel and set Bend Angle value to **0**. Now click Modifier in menu bar>

Parametric Deformers> Taper. Set Taper Curve to -4 to see the change. Taper parameters include the Amount and Curve, Primary and Effect Axes, and Limits. The Amount value defines the amount of taper applied to the affected end. The Curve value bends the taper inward for negative values or outward for positive values.

Twist modifier

The Twist modifier deforms an object by rotating one end of an axis in one direction and the other end in the opposite direction. Twist parameters include Angle and Bias values, a Twist Axis, and Limits. The Angle value is the amount of twist in degrees that is applied to the object. The Bias value causes the twists to bunch up near the Pivot Point for negative values or away from the Pivot Point for positive values.

Noise modifier

The Noise modifier randomly varies the position of object vertices in the direction of the selected axes. Noise parameters include Seed and Scale values, a Fractal option with Roughness and Iterations settings, Strength about each axis, and Animation settings. The Seed value sets the randomness of the noise. If two identical objects have the same settings and the same Seed value, they look exactly the same even though a random noise has been applied to them. If you alter the Seed value for one of them, then they will look dramatically different.

Stretch modifier

The Stretch modifier moves one axis in one direction while moving the other axes in the opposite direction, like pushing in on opposite sides of a balloon. Stretch parameters include Stretch and Amplify values, a Stretch Axis, and Limits. The Stretch value equates the distance the object is pulled, and the Amplify value is a multiplier for the Stretch value. Positive values multiply the effect, and negative values reduce the stretch effect.

Squeeze modifier

The Squeeze modifier takes the points close to one axis and moves them away from the center of the object while it moves other points toward the center to create a bulging effect. Squeeze parameters include Amount and Curve values for Axial Bulge and Radial Squeeze, and Limits and Effect Balance settings. The Effect Balance settings include a Bias value, which changes the object between the maximum Axial Bulge or the maximum Radial Squeeze. The Volume setting increases or decreases the volume of the object within the modifier's gizmo.

Push modifier

The Push modifier pushes an object's vertices inward or outward as if they were being filled with air. The Push modifier also has one parameter: the Push Value. This value is the distance to move with respect to the object's center. The positive Push value pushes the vertices outward away from the center, and a negative Push value pulls the vertices in towards the center. The Push modifier can increase the size of characters or make an object thinner by pulling its vertices in.

Relax modifier

The Relax modifier tends to smooth the overall geometry by separating vertices that lie closer than an average distance. Parameters include a Relax Value that is the percentage of the distance that the vertices move. Values can range between 1.0 and −1.0. A value of 0 has no effect on the object. Negative values have the opposite effect, causing an object to become tighter and more distorted. As you model, it is common for meshes to have sections that are too tight. The Relax modifier can be used to cause the areas that are too tight to be relaxed. Another common way to use the Relax modifier is to prepare surfaces for lighting using Radiosity. The Iterations value determines how many times this calculation is computed. The Keep Boundary Points Fixed option removes any points that are next to an open hole. Save Outer Corners maintains the vertex position of corners of an object.

Ripple modifier

The Ripple modifier creates ripples across the surface of an object. This modifier is best used on a single object; if several objects need a ripple effect, use the Ripple Space Warp. The ripple is applied via a gizmo that you can control. Parameters for this modifier include two Amplitude values and values for the Wave Length, Phase, and Decay of the ripple. The two amplitude values cause an increase in the height of the ripples opposite one another.

Lesson 19
Animate a waving flag using Wave modifier

Now your dream comes true. The much awaited steps of animation are given here by which you can create a waving flag. You must have seen your country's flag unfurling in the breeze on the theatre or computer screen. That is done using Wave modifier and animation. The Wave modifier produces a wave-like effect across the surface of the object.

(1) Go to NURBS Surfaces in Command panel> CV Surf and draw a surface in the viewport.

(2) With the surface selected, go to Modifiers> Parametric Deformers> Wave.

(3) In Parameters rollout set Amplitude 1 value to 10, Amplitude 2 value to 40, and Wave Length to 80. It should look like a flag shown in picture 5.0.

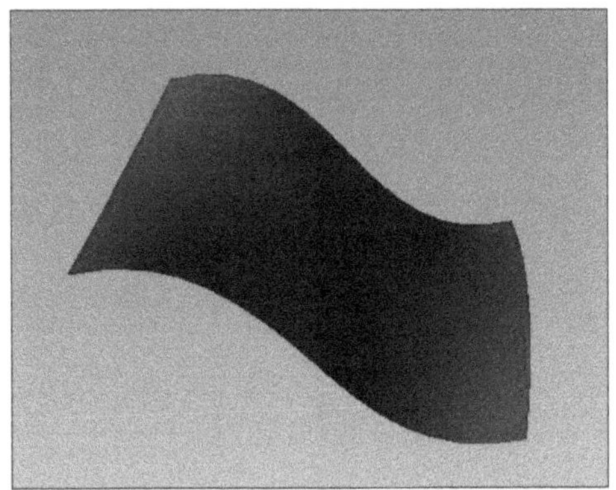

(4) Now you're going to animate the flag. With the object selected, just press the key N on your keyboard. The timeframe area at the bottom of the screen turns red. Drag the Time Slider in the timeframe to frame 100, and set the Phase value in Parameter rollout to 4. Press the Auto Key button (N) again to exit key mode.

(5) Click Animation in the Menu bar> Make Preview and click Create at the bottom of the next screen. That's it. You would see the animation video playing in your supported video player.

Picture 5.0

What is an Object-Space and World-Space modifier?

If you view the modifiers listed in the Modifier List (Command panel), they are divided into two categories: Object-Space and World-Space modifiers. Object-Space modifiers are modifiers that are applied to individual objects and that use the object's Local Coordinate System, so as the object is moved, the modifier goes with it. World-Space modifiers are based on World-Space coordinates instead of on an object's Local Coordinate System, so after a World-Space modifier is applied, it stays put, no matter where the object with which it is associated moves.

Skew modifier

The Skew modifier changes the tilt of an object by moving its top portion while keeping the bottom half fixed. Skew parameters include Amount and Direction values, a Skew Axis, and Limits.

Slice modifier

You can use the Slice modifier to divide an object into two separate objects. Applying the Slice modifier creates a Slice gizmo. This gizmo looks like a simple plane and can be transformed and positioned to define the slice location. To transform the gizmo, you need to select it from the Stack hierarchy. This modifier can help you make objects slowly disappear a layer at a time as well.

Shell modifier

When a mesh subobject is deleted, it leaves a hole in the surface that allows the inside of the object to be seen. This inside section doesn't have normals pointing the right direction, so the object appears blank unless the Force 2-Sided option in the Viewport Configuration dialog box is selected. The Shell modifier makes an object into a shell with a surface on the inside and outside of the object. For the Shell modifier, you can specify Inner and Outer Amount values. This is the distance from the original position that the inner or outer surfaces are moved. These values together determine how thick the shell is. The Bevel Edges and Bevel Spline options let you bevel the edges of the shell. By clicking on the Bevel Spline button, you can select a spline to define the bevel shape.

Spherify modifier

The Spherify modifier distorts an object into a spherical shape. The single Spherify parameter is the percent of the effect to apply. The Spherify modifier is different from the Push modifier; it can apply a bulge effect to a specific area, while the Push modifier moves all vertices equally outward for the entire object.

Lattice modifier

The Lattice modifier changes an object into a lattice by creating struts where all the edges are located or by replacing each joint with an object. The Lattice modifier considers all edges as struts and all vertices as joints.

Mirror modifier

You can use the Mirror modifier to create a mirrored copy of an object or subobject. The Parameters rollout lets you pick a mirror axis or plane and an Offset value. The Copy option creates a copy of the mirrored object and retains the original selection.

Displace modifier

The Displace modifier offers two unique sets of features. It can alter an object's geometry by displacing elements using a gizmo, or it can change the object's surface using a grayscale bitmap image. The Displace gizmo can have one of four different shapes: Planar, Cylindrical, Spherical, or Shrink Wrap. This gizmo can be placed exterior to an object or inside an object to push it from the inside. You can use the Displace modifier's gizmo as a modeling tool to change the surface of an object.

Preserve modifier

The Preserve modifier works to maintain Edge Lengths, Face Angles, and Volume as an object is deformed and edited. Before an object is modified, make an additional copy. Then edit one of the copies. To apply the Preserve modifier, click the Pick Original button; then click the unmodified object, and finally click the modified object. The object is modified to preserve the Edge Lengths, Face Angles, and Volume as defined in the Weight values. This helps prevent the topology of the modified object from becoming too irregular. The Iterations option determines the number of times the process is applied. You can also specify to apply to the Whole Mesh, to Selected Vertices Only, or to an Inverted Selection.

Substitute modifier

The Substitute modifier lets you place an object in the scene and substitute it with a higher resolution object during render time. The substitute object may come from with the scene or from an XRef file. To remove the substitute object, simply remove the Substitute modifier from the stack.

With all these modifiers explained in lesson 18 and 19, you can alter objects in a vast number of ways. Modifiers can work with every aspect of an object, including geometric deformations, materials, and general object maintenance.

Lesson 20
Modeling and Creativity

For a great majority of the people of the world the curiosity of learning Max is creating animated movies and games. One common use for 3D models is for games. Almost all the games are developed nowadays with Max. This includes PC games as well as console games for the XBox, Playstation, and Nintendo's

Game Cube. Autodesk is well aware of Max's position in the game industry and has made several additions to Max specifically for game developers, such as modifiers that can reduce the size of a mesh, the ability to paint vertices, and direct control over channel information. Another common modeling task that Max handles is architecture pre-visualization. To aid in the creation, Max includes the AEC Objects and a palette of architecture materials.

You can model an object in many ways. For example, you can make a mountain model out of primitive objects like blocks, cubes, and spheres, or you can create one as a polygon mesh. As your experience grows, you discover that some objects are easier to model using one method and some are easier using another. Max offers several different modeling types to handle various modeling situations. All geometric objects in Max can be divided into two general categories—parametric objects and editable objects. Parametric means that the geometry of the object is controlled by variables called parameters. Modifying these parameters modifies the geometry of the object. This powerful concept gives parametric objects lots of flexibility. For example, the sphere object has a parameter called Radius. Changing this parameter changes the size of the sphere. Parametric objects in Max include all the objects found in the Create menu. Editable objects do not have this flexibility of parameters, but they deal with subobjects and editing functions. The editable objects include Editable Spline, Mesh, Poly, Patch, and NURBS. Editable objects are listed in the Modifier Stack with the word Editable in front of their base object (except for NURBS objects, which are simply called NURBS Surfaces). For example, an editable mesh object is listed as Editable Mesh in the Modifier Stack. Editable objects aren't created; instead, they are converted or modified from another object. When a primitive object is converted to a different object type like an Editable Mesh or a NURBS object, it loses its parametric nature and can no longer be changed by altering its base parameters. Editable objects do have their advantages, though. You can edit subobjects such as vertices, edges, and faces of meshes—all things that you cannot edit for a parametric object. Each editable object type has a host of functions that are specific to its type.

Modeling types
The modeling types that you find in Max are:
1. Primitives: Basic parametric objects such as cubes, spheres, and pyramids. The primitives are divided into two groups consisting of Standard and Extended Primitives. The
AEC Objects are also considered primitive objects.
2. Shapes and splines: Simple vector shapes such as circles, stars, arcs, and text, and splines such as the Helix. These objects are fully renderable. The Create menu includes many parametric shapes and splines. These parametric objects can be converted to Editable Spline objects for more editing.
3. Polys: Objects composed of polygon faces, similar to mesh objects, but with unique features. These objects are also available only as Editable Poly objects.
4. Meshes: Complex models created from many polygon faces that are smoothed together when the object is rendered. These objects are available only as Editable Mesh objects.
5. Patches: Based on spline curves; patches can be modified using control points. The Create menu includes two parametric Patch objects, but most objects can also be converted to Editable Patch objects.
6. NURBS: Stands for Non-Uniform Rational B-Splines. NURBS are similar to patches in that they also have control points. These control points define how a surface spreads over curves.
7. Compound objects: A miscellaneous group of modeling types, including Booleans, loft objects, and scatter objects. Other compound objects are good at modeling one specialized type of object such as Terrain or BlobMesh objects.
8. Particle systems: Systems of small objects that work together as a single group. They are useful for creating effects such as rain, snow, and sparks.

9. <u>Hair and fur</u>: Modeling hundreds of thousands of cylinder objects to create believable hair would quickly bog down any system, so hair is modeled using a separate system that represents each hair as a spline.

10. <u>Cloth systems</u>: Cloth—with its waving, free-flowing nature—behaves like water in some cases and like a solid in others. Max includes a specialized set of modifiers for handling cloth systems.

Making objects editable

Here is what you have to understand before making an object editable. To create an editable object, you need to import it or convert it from another object type. You can convert objects by right-clicking on the object in the viewport and selecting the Convert To submenu from the pop-up quadmenu, or by right-clicking on the base object in the Modifier Stack and selecting the object type to convert to in the pop-up menu. Once converted, all the editing features of the selected type are available in the Modify panel, but the object is no longer parametric. The pop-up menu includes options to convert to editable mesh, editable poly, editable patch, and sometimes NURBS. If a shape or spline object is selected, then the object can also be converted to an editable spline. Using any of the Convert To menu options collapses the Modifier Stack. The Objects can be converted between the different types several times, but each conversion may subdivide the object. Therefore, multiple conversions are not recommended. Another way to convert objects is with the Turn to Poly, Turn to Mesh, or Turn to Patch modifiers. Converting an object by applying a modifier maintains the parametric nature of the original object, but doesn't give you access to the editable features.

Creating trumpet flowers

The saying "Practice makes a man perfect" is really true. When you do the tutorial, you will improve your knowledge, and you'll also understand the vivacity of Max. We're going to create a simple trumpet flower using several modeling types as each modeling type has its benefits. Let's try out the First way which is easy and simple.

<u>First way:</u>

 (1) To create a flower using the Editable Poly object, go to Create> Standard Primitives> Cylinder and drag in the Top viewport. Set the Radius to 40, the Height to 20, and the Cap Segments to 3.0. Right-click the Cylinder object, and select the Convert To> Editable Poly menu command from the pop-up quadmenu. Picture 5.1 shows the beautiful flower you're creating.

(2) In the Modifier Stack, select the Vertex subobject mode and select the center vertex in the Top viewport. In the Soft Selection rollout, click the Use Soft Selection option, and set the Falloff to 285 and the Pinch value to 2.5. Then drag the selected vertex downward in the Left viewport using Move tool. While transforming an object if you want to go from one viewport to another keeping the object or its part selected, you can do Ctrl+click in the next viewport.

(3) Select two middle rows of vertices in the Front viewport, disable the Soft Selection option, and scale the vertices down slightly to give the flower a bend. Then enable the Use NURMS Subdivision option in the Subdivision Surfaces rollout, and set the Iterations to 1. Click the Vertex subobject in the Modifier Stack to disable Vertex subobject mode.

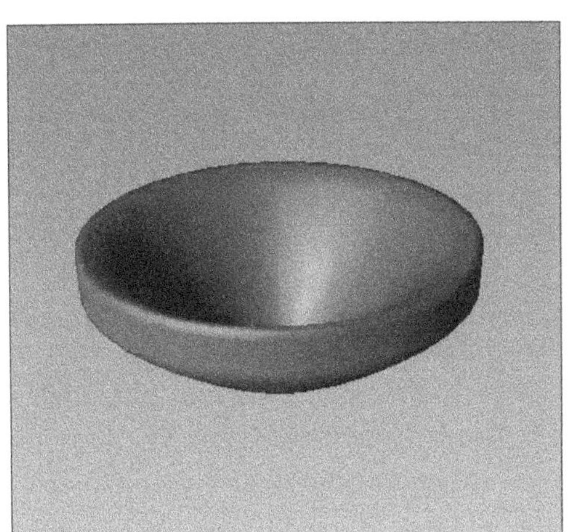

Picture 5.1

<u>Second way:</u>
(1) To create the same flower using patches, go to Create> Standard Primitives> Cylinder and drag in the top viewport to create another Cylinder object using the same settings. Right-click on the Cylinder object, and select the Convert To> Editable Patch menu command from the pop-up quadmenu.
(2) From the Modifier Stack, select Vertex subobject mode. Then select the center vertex, enable Soft Selection with the same settings, and drag in the Left viewport. Disable the Lock Handles option in the Selection rollout, select the Handle subobject mode, and drag the handles for the bottom vertex upward in both the Front and Left viewports until they make a sharp point at the bottom of the flower.

<u>Third way:</u>
(1) For the NURBS version of the flower, select the Create> NURBS> CV Curve and click in the Front viewport three times: at the bottom point of the flower, again about halfway up along the center axis, and again near the outer edge. These clicks form three control points that define the profile of the flower. You have to right-click to end the curve. Then right-click again on the curve, and select the Convert To> Convert to NURBS menu command from the pop-up menu.
(2) In the NURBS Creation Toolbox palette of tools that appears, click Create Lathe Surface and select the NURBS curve in the Front viewport. Set the Degrees value in the Lathe Surface rollout to 360, and then click on the Y Direction button and the Max Align button.

<u>Fourth way:</u>
(1) To create the same flower in fourth way, select Create> Shapes> Circle and create four circles centered about the same point in the Top viewport. Make their Radius values 1, 10, 20, and 40 respectively. Use the Select Objects dialog box (H) to select each circle in order and move it down in the Front viewport to its vertical position corresponding to the flower's profile.
(2) With the bottom circle selected, right-click and select the Convert To> Editable Spline menu command in the pop-up quadmenu. In the Geometry rollout, click Attach, select the other three circles in order, and right-click to exit attach mode. Then click Cross Section, and select each of the circles in order from the bottom upward. You have to right-click after you've selected all the circles and again to exit Cross Section mode. Select the Modifiers> Patch/Spline Editing> Surface menu command to apply a surface to the spline cage, and set the Patch Topology Steps value to 8.

Lesson 21
Understanding 2D and 3D
Within the 3D world, you frequently encounter flat surfaces—the side of a building, the top of a table, a billboard, and so on. All these objects have flat 2D surfaces. Understanding how objects are composed of 2D surfaces will help as you start to build objects in 3D.

Working in 2D in Max, you use two general objects: splines and shapes. A spline is a special type of line that curves according to mathematical principles. In Max, splines are used to create all sorts of shapes such as circles, ellipses, and rectangles. You can create splines and shapes using the Create> Shapes menu, which opens the Shapes category on the Create panel. Just as with the other categories, several spline-based shape primitives are available. Spline shapes can be rendered, but they are normally used to create more advanced 3D geometric objects by extruding or lathing the spline. You can even find a whole group of modifiers that apply to splines. You can use splines to create animation paths as well as Loft and NURBS objects, and you will find that splines and shapes, although they are only 2D, are used frequently in Max.

Shapes in Max are unique from other objects because they are drawn in 2D, which confines them to a single plane. That plane is defined by the viewport used to create the shape. For example, drawing a shape in the Top view constrains the shape to the XY plane, whereas drawing the shape in the Front view constrains it to the ZX plane. Even shapes drawn in the Perspective view are constrained to a plane such as the Home Grid. You usually produce 2D shapes in a drawing package like Adobe Illustrator or CorelDRAW. Max supports importing line drawings using the AI format.

The shape primitive buttons are displayed in the Object Type rollout of the Create panel when either the Create> Shapes or the Create> Extended Shapes menu is selected. The Shapes category include many basic shapes, including Line, Circle, Arc, NGon (a polygon where you can set the number of sides), Text, Section, Rectangle, Ellipse, Donut, Star, and Helix. The Extended Shapes category includes several shapes that are useful to architects, including WRectangle, Channel, Angle, Tee, and Wide Flange. You can use the Text primitive to add outlined text to the scene. In the Parameters rollout, you can specify a Font by choosing one from the drop-down list at the top of the Parameters rollout.

How 3D works?
Back to 3D again, I let you know how 3D works. First you need to know that Meshes (polygon meshes) are the most popular and the default model type for most 3D programs. You create them by placing polygonal faces next to one another so the edges are joined. The polygons can then be smoothed from face to face during the rendering process. Using meshes, you can create almost any 3D object, including simple primitives such as a cube or a realistic dinosaur. Meshes have lots of advantages. They are common, intuitive to work with, and supported by a large number of 3D software packages. In this chapter, you learn how to create and edit mesh and poly objects. The editing features available for the Editable Poly object are great for certain tasks, but they can be difficult to use for subtle deformations.
Instead, Max has another tool that makes simple deformations easy to complete—the Paint Deformation tool. Using this tool, you can add muscles on a flat character by painting over its surface. When an Editable Poly object is selected, three specific deformation brushes may be selected in the Paint Deformation rollout. Using these brushes, you can deform the surface of an object by dragging over the surface with the selected brush.

Using Selection rollout
The Selection rollout includes options for selecting subobjects. The By Vertex option is available in all but the Vertex subobject mode. It requires that you click a vertex in order to select an edge, border, polygon, or element. It selects all edges and borders that are connected to a vertex when the vertex is selected. The Ignore Backfacing option selects only those subobjects with normals pointing toward the current viewport. For example, if you are trying to select some faces on a sphere, only the faces on the side closest to you are selected. If this option is off, then faces on both sides of the sphere are selected. This option is helpful if many subobjects are on top of one another in the viewport. The Selection rollout also includes four buttons. These buttons include Shrink, Grow, Ring, and Loop. Use the Grow button to increase the current selection around the perimeter of the current selection and click the Shrink button to do the opposite.
The Ring and Loop buttons are available only in Edge and Border subobject modes. Use Ring and Loop to select all adjacent subobjects horizontally and vertically around the entire object. Ring selection looks for parallel edges, and Loop selection looks for all edges around an object that are aligned the same as the initial selection. For example, if you select a single edge of a sphere, the Ring button selects all edges going around the sphere and the Loop button selects all edges in a line from the top to the bottom of the sphere.

Modeling a clown head

In this tutorial you'll quickly deform a mesh sphere to create a clown face by selecting, moving, and working with some vertices.

(1) Go to Standard Primitives> Sphere, and drag in the Front viewport to create a sphere object. Then right-click the sphere, and select Convert To> Editable Mesh in the pop-up quadmenu.

(2) Click the plus sign of the Editable Mesh object in the Modifier Stack, and select Vertex. Enable the Ignore Backfacing option in the Selection rollout, and select the single vertex in the center of the Front

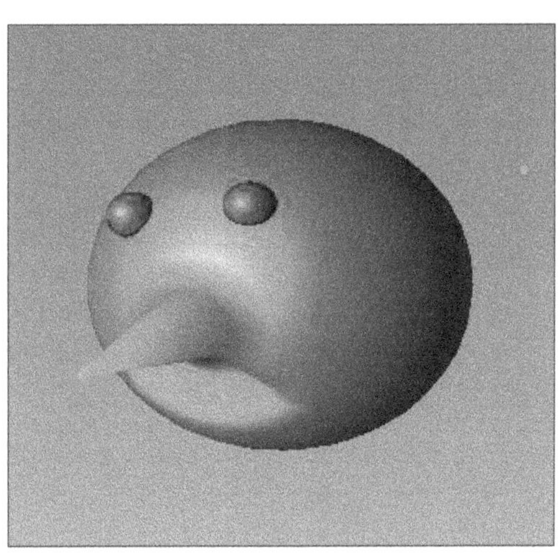

viewport. Make sure that the Select and Move button (W) is selected, and in the Left viewport, drag the vertex along the Z-axis until it projects from the sphere to become a long and pointy nose.

(3) To create the mouth, first zoom only the front viewport by taking zoom tool from bottom right corner, and then select several vertices in a circular arc below the nose. Holding down the Ctrl key makes selecting multiple vertices easy. Then move the selected vertices along the negative Z-axis in the Left viewport. See the picture 5.2 for help. This effect is useful also to bring smile on a 3D human-face.

(4) For the eyes, select Standard Primitives> Sphere and enable the AutoGrid option (just above the Sphere button). Then drag in the Front viewport to create two eyes.

Picture 5.2

Much of the power of editing meshes is contained within the Edit Geometry rollout. Features contained here include, among many others, the ability to create new subobjects, attach subobjects to the mesh, weld vertices, chamfer vertices, slice, explode, and align. In vertex subobject mode, using Delete and Break feature (the buttons in Geometry rollout) can be very fascinating.

Modeling a tooth

(1) Select Standard Primitives> Box, and drag in the Top viewport to create a Box object. Set its dimensions to 140 × 180 × 110 with Segments of 1 × 1 × 1. Then right-click, and select Convert To> Editable Poly from the pop-up quadmenu.

(2) Click the Polygon icon in the Selection rollout to enable Polygon subobject mode. Then select the Top viewport, and press B to change it to the Bottom viewport. Then click the box's bottom polygon in the Bottom viewport.

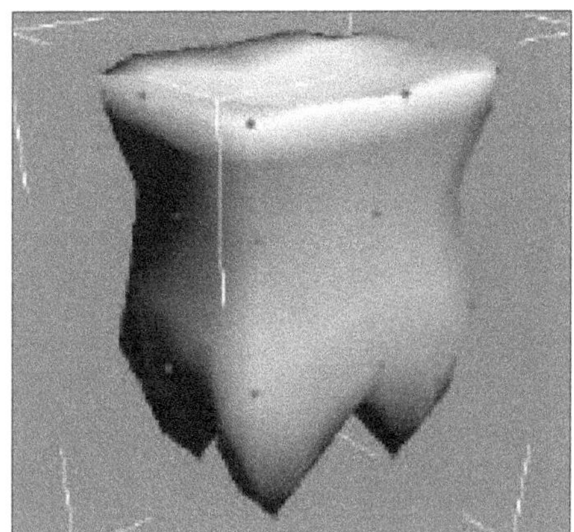

(3) Click the Select and Scale button (R), and scale the bottom polygon 10%. See the picture 5.3 for help.

(4) Drag over the entire object to select all polygons, and click the Tessellate button once to divide the polygon into more polygons. Then select Edit> Region> Window to enable the Window selection method, and drag over the bottom of the Box object in the Left viewport to select just the bottom polygons. Click the Tessellate button again.

(5) Select the Vertex subobject mode in the Selection rollout, press and hold the Ctrl key, and select the vertices at the center of each quadrant. Then move these vertices downward in the Left viewport a distance about equal to the height of the Box.

Picture 5.3

(6) Select the Bottom viewport again, and press T to change it back to the Top viewport. Select the single vertex in the center of the polygon with the Ignore Backfacing option enabled in the Selection rollout, and drag it slightly downward in the Left viewport.

(7) Disable the Ignore Backfacing option in the Selection rollout, and select the entire second row of vertices in the Left viewport. With the Select and Scale tool, scale these vertices toward the center in the polygon in the Top viewport.

(8) In the Subdivision Surface rollout, enable the Use NURMS Subdivision option and set the Iterations value to 1.

Painting deformations

The Paint Deformation feature is that it is available only for Editable Poly objects. When an Editable Poly object is selected, the Paint Deformation rollout appears at the very bottom of the Command Panel. At the top of the Paint Deformation rollout are three buttons used to select the type of deformation brush to use. These three brushes are the Push/Pull brush, the Relax brush, and the Revert brush. When one of these brushes is selected, the mouse cursor changes to a circular brush that follows the surface of the object as you move the mouse over the object. The Paint Deformation feature is very useful in adding surface details to organic objects such as the veins of a forearm.

MultiRes modifier

Creating a game requires a small file, and so, you can use the MultiRes modifier to create lower-resolution versions of a mesh object. This modifier is especially useful for creating real-time updated meshes for the gaming market. Once applied to a mesh object using the Modifier List in the Modify panel, you can set the desired options in the Generation Parameters section of the MultiRes Parameters rollout and click the Generate button to apply the MultiRes solution to the selected object.

Cap Holes modifier

The Cap Holes modifier patches any holes found in a geometry object. Sometimes when objects are imported, they are missing faces. This modifier can detect and eliminate these holes by creating a face along open edges. For example, if a spline is extruded and you don't specify Caps, then the extruded spline has holes at its end. The Cap Holes modifier detects these holes and creates a Cap. Cap Holes parameters include Smooth New Faces, Smooth with Old Faces, and Triangulate Cap. Smooth with Old Faces applies the same smoothing group as that used on the bordering faces.

Creating a NURBS leaf

(1) Select Create> NURBS> CV Surface, and in the Create Parameters rollout, increase the Length CVs to 6 and Width CVs to 6. Click the Generate Mapping Coords check box.

(2) In the Top viewport, click and drag to create the NURBS surface. In the Create Parameters rollout, set both the Length and Width to 180. While still in the Top viewport, rotate the NURBS surface 45 degrees along the Z-axis using the Select and Rotate tool so that it looks like a diamond shape.

(3) With the NURBS surface selected, open the Modify panel and click the plus sign to the left of the NURBS Surface object to gain access to the subobjects. Select the Surface CV subobject. The CV lattice is displayed in the Top viewport. See the picture 5.4 for help.

(4) Select the Non-Uniform Scale tool (R), constrain it to the X-axis (F5), and then drag-select the middle horizontal row of CVs. Scale them down (narrower) to 85 percent.

(5) Select the middle three horizontal rows of CVs (including the one just scaled), and scale them down to 90 percent. Then select the middle five horizontal rows, and scale them down to 90 percent. This step gently rounds the outside contours of the NURBS surface.

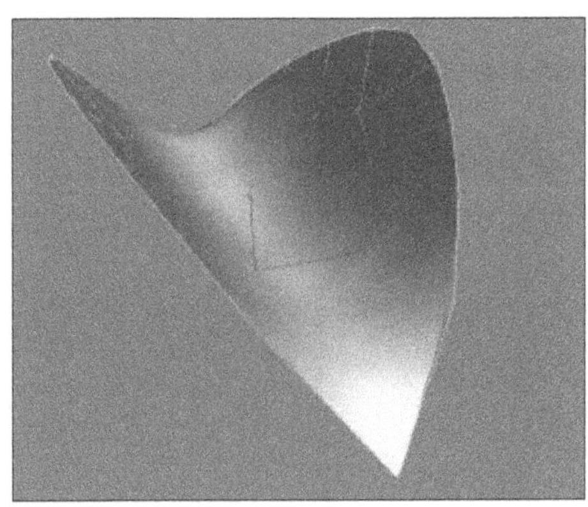

Picture 5.4

(6) In the Front viewport, you should see the edge of the NURBS surface. Maximize the viewport, and then select the Rotate tool, constrain it to the Z-axis, and select the right half of the CVs, but do not select the CVs at the very center. Rotate the CVs upward –60 degrees.

(7) Repeat the select-and-rotate process with the CV on the left half of the center, but do not alter the CVs at the very center. The leaf should now be U-shaped.

(8) Click the Move tool (W), constrain it to the Y-axis (F6), and then select the center row of CVs and move them downward – 40 units to make a deep V shape.

Lesson 22
Understanding Compound Objects
There is a lot to learn in Max and it needs a lot of practice. I understand that things are getting heavier and heavier but your patience with interest and creativity can take you miles ahead in your aspiration to become an animation artist.

Now we're talking about Compound Objects. The Compound Objects are two or more objects with the same number of vertices. Its subcategory includes several unique object types. You can access these object types with the Create> Compound menu or by clicking the Geometry category button in the Create panel and selecting Compound Objects in the subcategory drop-down list. All the object types included in the Compound Objects subcategory are displayed as buttons at the top of the Create panel.

Morph: Consists of two or more objects with the same number of vertices. The vertices are interpolated from one object to the other over several frames.

Scatter: Randomly scatters a source object about the scene. You can also select a Distribution object that defines the volume or surface where the objects scatter.

Conform: Wraps the vertices of one object onto another. You can use this option to simulate a morph between objects with different numbers of vertices.

Connect: Connects two objects with open faces by joining the holes with additional faces.

BlobMesh: Creates a metaball object that flows from one object to the next like water.

ShapeMerge: It embeds a spline into a mesh object or subtracts the area of a spline from a mesh object.

Boolean: Created by performing Boolean operations on two or more overlapping objects. The operations include Union, Subtraction, Intersection, and Cut.

Terrain: Creates terrains from the elevation contour lines like those found on topographical maps.

Loft: Sweeps a cross-section shape along a spline path.

Mesher: Creates an object that converts particle systems into mesh objects as the frames progress. This makes assigning modifiers to particle systems possible.

Creating particles
A particle is a small, simple object that is duplicated en masse, like snow, rain, or dust. Just as in real life, Max includes many different types of particles that can vary in size, shape, texture, color, and motion. These different particle types are included in various particle systems. You can find all the various particle systems under the Create panel and also in the Create menu. To access these systems, click the Geometry category and select the Particle Systems subcategory from the drop-down list. All the particle systems then appear as buttons. Or you can select the Create> Particles menu. With the Particle Systems

subcategory selected, click the button for the type of particle system that you want to use and then click in a viewport to create the particle system emitter icon. The emitter icon is a gizmo that looks like a plane or a sphere and that defines the location in the system where the particles all originate. Attached to the icon is a single line indicates the direction in which the particles move when generated. This line points by default toward the construction grid's negative Z-axis when first created.

Spray: Simulates drops of water. These drops can be Drops, Dots, or Ticks. The particles travel in a straight line from the emitter's surface after they are created.

Snow: Similar to the Spray system, with the addition of some fields to make the particles Tumble as they fall. You can also render the particles as Six Pointed shapes that look like snowflakes.

Blizzard: An advanced version of the Snow system that can use the same mesh object types as the Super Spray system. Binding the system to the Wind Space Warp can create storms.

PArray: Can use a separate Distribution Object as the source for the particles. For this system, you can set the particle type to Fragment and bind it to the PBomb Space Warp to create explosions.

PCloud: Confines all generated particles to a certain volume. A good use of this system is to reproduce bubbles in a glass or cars on the road.

Super Spray: An advanced version of the Spray system that can use different mesh objects, closely packed particles called MetaParticles, or an instanced object as its particles. Super Spray is useful for rain and fountains. Binding it to the Path Follow Space Warp can create waterfalls.

Particle Flow Source: Particles that can be defined using the Particle Flow window and controlled using actions and events.

Creating a black hole using Particle Flow

Particle systems are one of the best sources for special effects, and with the Particle Flow interface, you can control them more easily. In this tutorial, we create an array of particle systems and have all their particles flow together to form a black hole.

(1) Go to Create> Particles> Particle Flow Source, and drag in the Left viewport to create the icon. The icon's direction arrow should point to the right in the Top viewport. With the icon selected, click the Affect Pivot Only button in the Hierarchy panel and move the icon to the origin location in the Top viewport. Then click the Affect Pivot Only button again to disable pivot mode.

(2) Go to Create> Standard Primitives> Sphere, and create a small sphere in the Top viewport at the grid origin in the center of the viewport.

(3) Click the Animation Auto Key (N), and at the bottom of the interface drag the Time Slider to frame 100. Then select the sphere object in the Left viewport, and move it downward a little. Then select the Particle Flow Source icon in the Top viewport, and rotate it about 60 degrees. Then press N again to disable the Auto Key and leave animation mode. See picture 5.5 for help.

(4) With the Particle Flow icon selected, click the Particle View button in the Modify panel (or press the 6 key) to open the Particle Flow window. Select the Birth event, and change the Emit Stop value to 100 and the Amount to 200. Select the Shape event, and change the Shape to Sphere and the Size value to 2.0. In the Display event, change the Visible % to 10.

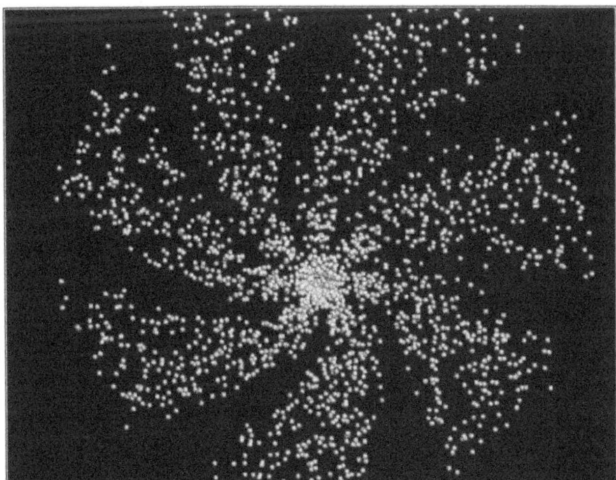

Picture 5.5

(5) Drag the Speed by Surface event from the Depot window, and drop it on top of the Speed event in the Event node. Select the Control Speed Continuously option from the drop-down list, enable the Speed option, and set the Speed value to 100 and the Speed Variation to 20. Then click the Add button, and select the small Sphere object in the Top viewport.

(6) Select the Particle Flow icon; with the Shift key held down, rotate the icon about 52 degrees and enter 6 for the Number of Copies in the Clone Options dialog box that appears. This creates particle flow icons that surround and feed the black hole.

Working with Hair

The way Max deals with hair is unique and needs some explanation. Hair, like particle systems, deals with thousands of small items. In Max, hair doesn't exist as geometry, but is applied to scene objects as a separate modifier. This level of separation keeps the hair solution independent of the geometry and makes removing the hair solution as needed easy. It also keeps the viewport display from bogging down. The Hair and Fur modifier is a World-Space Modifier (WSM), meaning that it is applied using the World Space coordinates instead of local ones. The other half of the Hair and Fur solution is a render effect that allows the hair to be rendered. This render effect is applied and configured automatically when the Hair and Fur modifier is applied to an object. This causes the scene with hair to be rendered in two passes. The geometry is rendered first, followed by the hair.

To apply hair you go to Modifiers> Hair and Fur> Hair and Fur WSM. After hair is applied to an object, you can use the parameters in the Modify panel to change the hair's properties. If you want to localize the hair growth to a specific area of the object, you can make a subobject selection using the controls in the Selection rollout. The available subobjects include Face, Polygon and Element. After making a subobject selection, click the Update Selection to display the guide hairs only in the selected area in the viewports. The Display rollout includes settings for controlling how many hairs are displayed in the viewports. You can select to display Guide Hairs and actual hairs and set a color for each. You can also select a Percentage value of the total hairs to display in the viewport up to the number in the Max Hairs value. Applying hair to a single spline doesn't create any hair, but if multiple splines are included as part of the same Editable Spline object, then the hair is interpolated between the various splines in the order they are attached following the spline's curvature. There are several style buttons and Hair and Fur Presets dialog box that you'll love to use. The hair displayed in the viewport is only a fraction of it. To see all the hairs, you need to render the scene as you have rendered long back in lesson 5.

Creating a snowman with hair

(1) To create a snowman, go to Standard Primitives> GeoSphere and draw a white sphere in viewport. Make a clone of this object and place the clone above the first sphere. Use Scale tool to make second sphere a litter smaller. Make one more clone and place it above the second sphere making it smaller than second.

(2) Select top sphere, right-click on it and select Convert to Editable Mesh. Select Vertex mode in Modifier stack by clicking + sign of Editable Mesh. Select the vertex in the center of the sphere, put check mark on Ignore Backfacing in Selection rollout, and use Move tool to drag selected vertex to make a nose of the snowman. After nose is created, get out of vertex mode by clicking on Vertex in the stack. See the picture 5.6, but if you're good in design, you can create better than what is shown.

Picture 5.6

(3) Click GeoSphere again, enable AutoGrid which is just above GeoSphere button, and draw two black eyes of the snowman.

(4) Now to create hair of the snowman, with top sphere selected, go to Modifier> Hair and Fur> Hair and Fur and in General Parameters, set Hair Count: 20000, Hair Segments: 100, Cut Length: 100, uncheck Interpolate option, and under Display rollout select Hair Color: Black. That's it. Click Rendering> Render> Render to view hair.

Understanding a Cloth System

If you drop a shirt over a chair, how does it land? It folds and bunches as it drapes over the solid object. Also notice how different types of cloth drape differently. Compare how silk reacts verses a terry-cloth towel. Being able to accurately simulate how cloth reacts to scene objects and forces is yet another critical element that can really make a difference in your final scenes. With a plane primitive, you can easily create a perfectly straight blanket, towel, or flag. Max also has a separate stand-alone cloth simulation system aptly named Cloth that you can use not only to create deformable cloth, but to animate it as well. When you start to model a cloth object, keep in mind that the model must have enough resolution so that it can accurately fold over itself several times. If the resolution isn't defined enough, then the bending of the cloth is not believable. You can increase the resolution of a model in several ways. The Garment Maker modifier includes parameters that can increase the resolution of a mesh, or you can use the HSDS modifier to increase an object's resolution. By the way the easiest way to create cloth panels is to draw the entire cloth panel and then use the Break Vertex command in Vertex subobject mode to break each corner.

Using Garment Maker to define cloth

Clothes can be added to models using a method that is similar to the way real clothes are made. Each section of cloth, called a panel, is outlined using lines and splines. Include a break at each corner of the panel or the modifier will round the corner. After you have all the various panels created, you can apply the Modifiers> Cloth> Garment Maker to each panel and set its Density value. The next step is to position the panels so they surround the model that they will be draped over. You can do this manually or by using Panel Position align buttons in the Panels rollout that appears in Panels subobject mode. With the panels in place you can stitch seams between the panels using the Curves subobject mode for flat drawn panels or using the Seams subobject mode for panels that are positioned about a model. After the seams are defined, you can apply the Modifiers> Cloth> Cloth modifier to pull the panels together and simulate the cloth's motion.

Creating a cloth on bamboo-sticks

Here is what is going to blow you off! The scene of this tutorial would look so real that you'll start clapping on your own creation. First time when I created, I couldn't believe that that was my creation. What happens that any geometry object can be made into a cloth object using the Cloth modifier available by selecting the Modifiers> Cloth> Cloth menu command. Although the modifier is added to the object, it is set to Inactive by default. To activate the cloth, you need to open the Object Properties dialog box. The Modifiers> Cloth menu also includes a Garment Maker modifier that is used to create cloth objects from 2D panels that are stitched together.

(1) To create a bamboo first, go to Standard Primitives> Tube and draw it on the left side in Perspective viewport. In Parameters: set Radius 1 to 2.0, Radius 2 to 1.5, and Height to 40. Make a clone of it and drag the clone object on the right side in the viewport. Draw one more tube, set Radius value same but

increase the height and place it at the top of these two sticks using Move and Rotate tools. You may have to work hard in all the viewports to place it correctly.

(2) Choose Create> Standard Primitives> Plane and drag to create a plane object. Set the Length and Width Segment values to 100 to make the sufficient resolution for the cloth, and drag the plane object upward so it sits above the stick. See picture 5.7 for help.

(3) With the plane object selected, choose Modifiers> Cloth> Cloth menu command to apply the Cloth modifier to the object. Open the Modifier panel, and click the Object Properties button in the Object rollout to open the Object Properties dialog box. Select the Plane01 object in the left list, and choose the Cloth option. Then select the Silk option from the Presets drop-down list, and set the Thickness to 0.5.

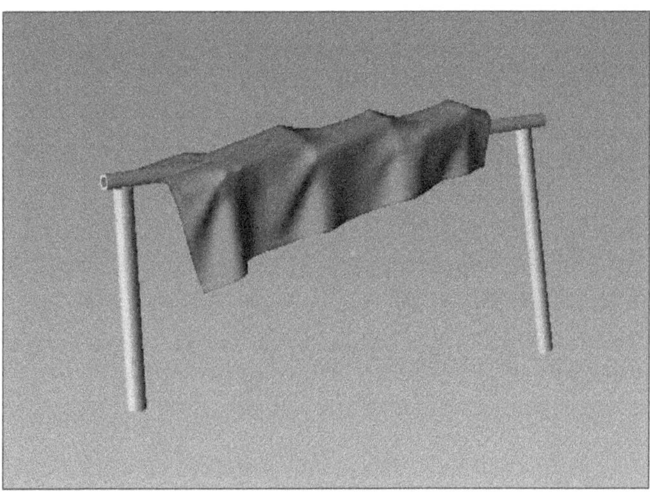

(4) With the Object Properties dialog box still open, click the Add Objects button, select the All button, and click the Add button. With all added properties in the left list selected, choose the Collision Object option and click the OK button to close the dialog box.

(5) In the Simulation Parameters rollout, enable the End Frame option and set the end frame to 100. Then click the Simulate button in the Object rollout. The plane object descends and covers the sticks being draped as it falls. It has created an animation in the background as well. To get blown off, click Animation> Make Preview> Create.

Picture 5.7

Lesson 23
The functions of Material Editor
The Material Editor can add a whole new level of realism using materials that simulate many different types of physical properties. It is used to dress, color, and paint objects. Just as materials in real life can be described as scaly, soft, smooth, opaque, or blue, materials applied to 3D objects can mimic properties such as color, texture, transparency, shininess, and so on. Many of these material properties are not visible until the scene is rendered. Within the Material Editor are several different color swatches that control different aspects of the object's color.

Ambient: Defines an overall background lighting that affects all objects, including the color of the object when it is in shadows. This color can be locked to the Diffuse color so that they are changed together.

Diffuse: The surface color of the object surface in normal, full light. The normal color of an object is typically defined by its Diffuse color.

Specular: The color of the highlights where the light is focused on the surface of a shiny material.

Self-Illumination: The color that the object glows from within. It takes over any shadows on the object.

Filter: The transmitted color caused by light shining through a transparent object.

Reflect: The color reflected by a raytrace material to other objects in the scene.

Luminosity: Causes an object to glow with the defined color. It is similar to Self-Illumination color but can be independent of the Diffuse color.

Opacity and transparency
Opaque objects are objects that you cannot see through, such as rocks and trees. Transparent objects, on the other hand, are objects that you can see through, like glass and clear plastic. Max's materials

include several controls for adjusting these properties, including Opacity and several Transparency controls. Opacity is the amount that an object refuses to allow light to pass through it. It is the opposite of transparency and is typically measured as a percentage. An object with 0 percent opacity is completely transparent, and an object with opacity of 100 percent doesn't let any light through. Transparency is the amount of light that is allowed to pass through an object. Because this is the opposite of opacity, transparency can be defined by the opacity value. Several options enable you to control transparency, including Falloff, Amount, and Type.

Reflection and refraction

A reflection is what you see when you look in the mirror. Shiny objects reflect their surroundings. By defining a material's reflection values, you can control how much it reflects its surroundings. A mirror, for example, reflects everything, but a rock won't reflect at all. Refraction is the bending of light as it moves through a transparent material. The amount of refraction that a material produces is expressed as a value called the Index of Refraction. The Index of Refraction is the amount that light bends as it goes through a transparent object. For example, a diamond bends light more than a glass of water, so it has a higher Index of Refraction value. The default Index of Refraction value is 1.0 for objects that don't bend light at all. Water has a value of 1.3; glass a value of around 1.5, and solid crystal a value of around 2.0. Reflection Dimming controls how much of the original reflection is lost as the surroundings are reflected within the scene.

Shininess and specular highlights

Shiny objects, such as polished metal or clean windows, include highlights where the lights reflect off their surfaces. These highlights are called specular highlights and are determined by the Specular settings. These settings include Specular Level, Glossiness, and Soften values. The Specular Level is a setting for the intensity of the highlight. The Glossiness determines the size of the highlight: Higher values result in a smaller highlight. The Soften value thins the highlight by lowering its intensity and increasing its size. A rough material has the opposite properties of a shiny material and almost no highlights. The Roughness property sets how quickly the Diffuse color blends with the Ambient color. Cloth and fabric materials have a high Roughness value; plastic and metal Roughness values are small.

Using Material Editor

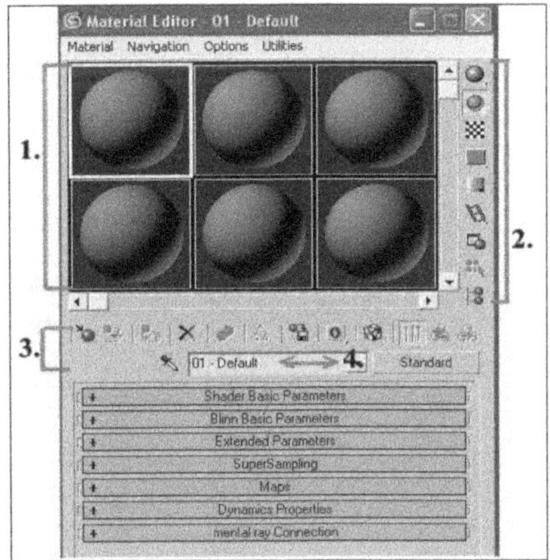

You can access the Material Editor by choosing Rendering> Material Editor, or clicking the Material Editor Button on the main toolbar (it has four small rendered spheres on the icon), or using the M keyboard shortcut. At the top of the default Material Editor Window is a menu of options including Material, Navigation, Options, and Utilities. The menu commands found in these menus offer the same functionality as the toolbar buttons, but the menus are often easier to find than the buttons. The picture 5.8 shows the area and set of buttons of Material Editor in which 1 = Sample slots area, 2 = Vertical buttons, 3 = Horizontal buttons, and 4 = Material name. You can use this window to create, store, and work with materials.

Picture 5.8

In **Vertical buttons** (numbered 2 in the picture), the <u>first button</u> is Sample Type which has three flyout buttons - Sphere, Cylinder, and Box. The <u>second button</u> is Backlight that lets you turn backlighting in the selected sample slot on or off. The <u>third button</u> is Background that displays a checkered background image or a custom background behind the material, which is helpful when displaying a transparent material. The fourth button is Sample UV Tiling which sets UV tiling for the map in the sample slot. The default is 1×1. Additional options available as flyouts are 2 × 2, 3 × 3, and 4 × 4. This setting affects only maps. The fifth button is Video Color Check that checks the current material for colors that are unsupported by the NTSC and PAL formats. The sixth button is Make Preview which is used to generate, view, and save material preview renderings. The seventh button is Options which opens the Material Editor Options dialog box. This dialog box includes settings for enabling material animation, loading a custom background, defining the light intensity and color, and number of sample slots. The eighth button is Select by Material which selects all objects using the current material. This button opens the Select Objects dialog box with those objects selected. The ninth button is Material/Map Navigator which opens the Material/Map Navigator dialog box. This dialog box displays a tree of all the levels for the current material.

In **Horizontal buttons** (numbered 3 in the picture), the first button is Get Material which opens the Material/Map Browser for selecting materials. The second button is Put Material in Scene which updates the materials applied to objects in the viewport after materials have been edited. The third button is Assign Material Selection which paints the selected object with the selected material. The fourth button is Reset Map/Mtl to Default Settings which removes any modified properties and resets the material properties to their defaults. The fifth button is Make Material Copy which creates a copy of the current material in the selected sample slot. The sixth button is Make Unique which makes instanced materials into a new stand-alone material. The seventh button is Put to Library which opens a simple dialog box that lets you rename the material and saves it into the current open library. The eighth button is Material Effects Channel that sets a unique channel ID for applying post-processing effects. This button includes channels 1–15 as flyouts. A material with channel 0 means that no effect will be applied. The ninth button is Show Map in Viewport that displays 2D material maps on objects in the viewports. The tenth button is Show End Result that displays the material in the sample slot with all levels applied. If this button is disabled, you will see only the level that is currently selected. The next button is Go to Parent which moves up one level for the current material. This applies only to compound objects with several levels. The next button is Go Forward to Sibling which selects the next map or material at the same level. The next button is Pick Material From Object which enables you to select a material from an object in the scene and load the material into the selected sample slot. The next button is Material drop-down list that lists the elements in the current material. You can change the material or map name by typing a new name in this field. The next button is Type button which displays the current material or map type that is being used. Clicking this button opens the Material/Map Browser where you can select a new material or map type.

Using the sample slots
The Material Editor includes 24 sample slots that display materials and map examples. Each of these sample slots contains one material or map. Only one sample slot can be selected at a time and the selected slot is outlined with a white border. Sample slots are temporary placeholders for materials and maps. An actual scene can have hundreds of materials. By loading a material into a sample slot, you can change its parameters, apply it to other materials, or save it to a library for use in other scenes. When a file is saved, all materials in the Material Editor are saved with the file.
When you select a material, you can apply it to the selected object in the viewports with the Assign Material to Selection button (the third button from the left on the horizontal toolbar under the sample slots) or with the Material> Assign to Selection menu command. Alternatively, you can drag a material from its sample slot and drop it on an object. When you assign a material to an object in the scene, the

material becomes "Hot." A Hot material is automatically updated in the scene when the material parameters change. Hot materials have white corner brackets displayed around their sample slots. You can "cool" a material by clicking the Copy Material button (the fifth from the left) or choosing Material> Make Material Copy menu command. This detaches the sample slot from the material in the scene to which it is applied, so that any changes to the material aren't applied to the object. Whenever a material is applied to an object in the scene, the material is added to a special library of materials that get saved with the scene. Materials do not need to be loaded in one of the sample slots to be in the scene library. You can also load materials into the scene library that aren't applied to an object using the Put Material to Scene button (the second button from the left) or the Material> Put to Scene menu command. You can see all the materials included in the scene library in the Material/Map Browser by selecting the Scene radio button. In addition to the scene library, you can also put materials into a separate material library. The Put to Library button (the seventh from the left) or the Material> Put to Library menu command places the current selected material into the default library. Clicking the Get Material button opens the Material/Map Browser where you can see the current library by clicking the Material Library radio button.

Another useful option is obtaining a material from an object in the scene. Clicking the eyedropper button to the left of the Material Name or choosing the Material> Pick from Object menu command changes the cursor to an eyedropper. You can then click an object in one of the viewports, and the object's material is loaded into the current sample slot.

Setting Material Editor Options
You open the Material Editor Options dialog box by clicking the Options button to the right of the sample slots, selecting Options from the Options menu, right-clicking the pop-up menu, or by just pressing the O key. The Material Editor Options dialog box includes options that control how the materials are displayed in the sample slots. These options are as follows:

Manual Update: Doesn't update any changes in the sample slot until the slot is clicked on.
Don't Animate: Causes materials not to animate when an animation is played or the Time Slider is dragged. It does, however, update these materials to the current frame.
Animate Active Only: Animates only the active sample slot if it contains an animated material. This option isn't available when the Don't Animate option is selected.
Update Active Only: Updates only the active sample slot when changes are made to the material.
Antialias: Enables anti-aliasing for all sample slots. Aliasing is a negative staircase-type effect that occurs for pixel-based images when adjacent pixels along the edges of an image are different colors. Anti-aliasing is a process for eliminating this distracting effect and smoothing the edges.
Progressive refinement: Causes materials to be rendered progressively. This causes the material to appear quickly as blocky sections and then slowly in more detail. This gives you a rough idea of how the material looks before the rendering is finished.
Simple Multi Display Below Top Level: Displays several different areas for only the top level when a Multi/Sub-Object material is applied.
Display Maps as 2D: Displays stand-alone maps in 2D and not on the sample object. This feature helps you to know when you're looking at a map versus a material.
Custom Background: Enables you to use a custom background behind the sample slots. You can load the background using the button to the right of the option. Once changed, the new background is used in all sample slots where the background is enabled.

Display Multi/Sub-object Material Propagation Warning: Lets you to disable the warning screen that appears when you apply a Multi/Sub-object Material to an instanced object.

Auto-Select Texture Map Size: Automatically scales Real-World textures on the sample sphere so that they appear correctly.

Use Real-World Map Size for Geometry Samples: Causes all textures displayed within the sample slots to use Real-World mapping coordinates. This option is available when the Auto-Select Texture Map Size option is disabled.

Coloring Easter eggs

(1) Draw four white-color spheres in the viewport and give them the shape of eggs using Transformation (Move, Scale and Rotate) tools.

Picture 5.9

(2) Open the Material Editor by choosing Rendering> Material Editor and increase the number of sample slots by right-clicking the active material and selecting 5 × 3 Sample Windows from the pop-up menu (or press the X key). See the picture 5.9 for help.

(3) Select the first sample slot, and click the Diffuse color swatch in the rollout below it. From the Color Selector that appears, drag the cursor around the color palette until you find the color you want and then click Close.

(4) In any viewport, select an egg and then click the Assign Material to Selection button in the Material Editor, or you can simply drag the material from its sample slot to the viewport object. Repeat Steps 3 and 4 for all the eggs.

Lesson 24

Using the Standard Material

Standard materials are the default Max material type. They provide a single, uniform color determined by the Ambient, Diffuse, Specular, and Filter color swatches. Standard materials can use any one of several different shaders. Shaders are algorithms used to compute how the material should look, given its parameters. These tools include an image-editing package such as Photoshop, a digital camera, and a scanner. With these tools, you can create and capture bitmap images that can be applied as materials to the surface of the object. Standard materials also have parameters for controlling highlights, opacity, and self-illumination. Standard materials include the following rollouts: Shader Basic Parameters, Basic Parameters (based on the shader type), Extended Parameters, SuperSampling, Maps, Dynamic Properties, and mental ray connection. By modifying these parameters, you can create really unique materials. With all the various rollouts, even a standard material has an infinite number of possibilities.

Multi-Layer shader

This is just an example of what you can do. The Multi-Layer shader includes two Anisotropic highlights. Each of these highlights can have a different color. All parameters for this shader are the same as the Anisotropic shader described previously, except that there are two Specular Layers and one additional parameter: Roughness. The Roughness parameter defines how well the Diffuse color blends into the Ambient color. When Roughness is set to a value of 0, an object appears the same as with the Blinn shader, but with higher values, up to 100, the material grows darker. Picture 6.0 shows several materials with a Multi-Layer shader applied. The first two images have two specular highlights each with an orientation value of 60 and Anisotropy values of 60 and 90. The third image has an increased Specular Level of 110 and a decrease in the Glossiness to 10. The fourth image has a change in the Orientation value for one of the highlights to 20, and the final image has a drop in the Anisotrophy value to 10. Like this, you can create many materials of your own.

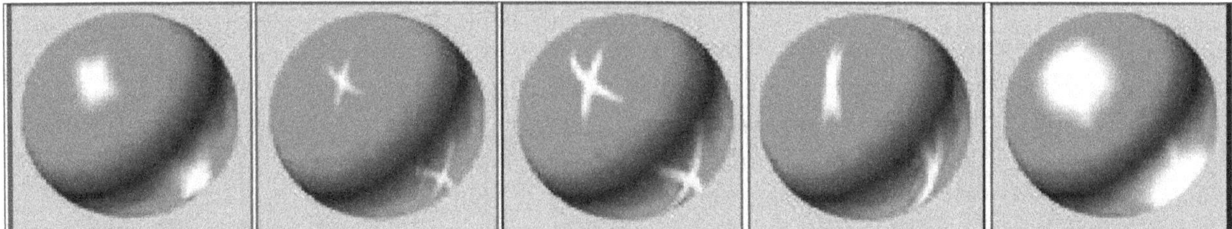

Picture 6.0

Using External Tools

Several external tools can be valuable when you create material textures. These tools can include an image-editing program like Photoshop, a digital camera or camcorder, and a scanner. With these tools, you can create or capture images that can be applied as maps to a material using the map channels. After the image is created or captured, you can apply it to a material by clicking a map shortcut button or by selecting a map in the Maps rollout. This opens the Material/Map Browser, where you can select the Bitmap map type and load the image file from the file dialog box that appears. Using Photoshop's

filters enables you to quickly create a huge variety of textures that add life and realism to your textures. Digital cameras and camcorders are inexpensive enough that they really are a necessary item when creating material textures. Although Photoshop can be used to create many unique and interesting textures, a digital image of riverbed stones is much more realistic than anything that can be created with Photoshop. The world is full of interesting textures that can be used in creating images. Picture 6.1 shows some beautiful materials that you can create using external tools.

Picture 6.1

Using Compound Materials

Now it'll definitely surprise you that you can create Compound materials also which combine several different materials into one. You select a compound object type by clicking the Type button in the Material Editor and then selecting the material type from the Material/Map Browser. The Type button is the button to the right of the material name. It lists the current material on the button, such as Standard, which is the default material. Most of the entries in the Material/Map Browser are compound objects. Whenever compound materials are selected, the Replace Material dialog box appears, asking whether you want to discard the current material or make the old material a submaterial. This feature enables you to change a normal material into a compound material while retaining the current material. Compound materials usually include several different levels. For example, a Top/Bottom material includes a separate material for the top and the bottom. Each of these submaterials can then include another Top/Bottom material, and so on. The Material/Map Navigator dialog box (accessed by clicking the Material/Map Navigator button) displays the material as a hierarchical list. This list lets you easily choose the level you want to work with.

Creating Baked Textures and Normal Maps

3D games create interactive scenes that are displayed in real-time with the highest quality graphics. To achieve this, game developers use a number of tricks designed to speed up the rendering time. One of these tricks is prerendering textures and applying these pre-rendered textures as texture maps. The process of applying pre-rendered textures as maps is called baking a texture. Rendering textures is a significant part of the rendering process, and baking a texture doesn't remove this step; it simply completes the step beforehand, so that the game engine doesn't need to do the texture calculations. Another common efficiency trick is to apply colors as vertex colors. By applying vertex colors, the model keeps track of the color value for each vertex in a mesh. Vertex colors are so efficient that a single model can include multiple sets of vertex colors and each set is stored in a channel that can be changed as needed by the game engine. For example, one channel can include the colors for a new car model with a shiny new paint job and another channel can be used as the car is damaged later in the game.

When 3D models are used in games, the color and material data for the model is stored in channels. The game engine then knows if it wants to change the color of a group of vertices because of an explosion that has happened, it just looks in the preset channel, finds the vertices it needs, changes the color, and then goes on with the game. Working with channels is a very efficient way to interface with the gaming engine, but a sloppy game developer can introduce a model to the game engine with all sorts of unneeded or exaggerated channels. If this happens, the game engine can ignore the extra channels and get the wrong information, which can cause your hero to march off into battle without a weapon. Worse, it can crash the system. To prevent problems and to streamline the number of channels that are included with game models, Max includes a Map Channel Info editor that you can use to manipulate the various channel data. This editor can be opened using the Tools> Channel Info menu command.

The Map Channel Info dialog box shows lots of information including the Object Name; its ID; its Channel Name; the number of Vertices, Faces, and Dead Vertices; and its Size. With this information, you can quickly determine which channels are taking up the most space and eliminate them. All objects include some default channels for mesh, which holds the geometry; vsel, which holds the selected vertices; -2:Alpha, which holds the alpha channel information; -1:Illum, which holds illumination values; and channel 0:vc, which holds vertex color information. Objects also include at least one default map channel (even if it is empty). These channels cannot be deleted. The interface lets you Copy and Paste selected channels. You can give each channel a name with the Name button. Beneath the Copy button, text appears that lists the information currently copied in the Copy Buffer. Channels can be copied only between channels that have the same number of vertices. The Clear button clears out the selected channels, but you cannot clear a map channel if there is another map channel above it. The Add button adds a new map channel to the object. Objects can hold as many as 99 map channels. The Clear and Add buttons also apply UVW Mapping Clear or UVW Mapping Add modifiers to the Modifier Stack. The Paste command also adds a modifier.

These modifiers are convenient because they can easily be removed or reordered in the Stack. If changes have been made in the Modifier Stack, the Update button reflects these changes in the Map Channel Info dialog box. The SubComp button shows the channel components if they exist. For example, map channels can be broken into X, Y, and Z components, and other channels like Alpha have R, G, and B components. The Lock button holds the current channels even if another object is selected. After new channels have been created, you can recall them at any time using the Select by Channel modifier. This modifier is in the Create> Selection Modifiers> Select by Channel menu command. Using this modifier, you can choose to Replace, Add, or Subtract a given channel from the selection. The available channels for the selection are listed by their channel name in drop-down list.

Rendering to a Texture

One common way to speed game calculations is to pre-render the textures used in a game and then to save these textures as texture maps. The texture map takes more memory to save, but can greatly speed the rendering time required by the game engine. This process of pre-rendering a texture is called texture baking. Texture baking can be accomplished in Max using the Rendering> Render to Texture menu command (or by pressing the 0 key). This opens the Render to Texture dialog box. In several ways, the Render to Texture dialog box resembles the Render Scene dialog box, including a Render button at the bottom edge of the interface. To create a baked texture, select a Texture Element from the Output rollout and click the Render button. Clicking the Render button creates the baked texture for the selected object and saves it in the directory specified in the General Settings rollout. It also applies an Automatic Flatten UVs modifier to the Modifier Stack and applies a Shell material to the object. The Shell material contains the object's original material along with the new baked material. You can select which material is displayed in the Viewport and which is rendered using the options to the bottom right of the Render to Texture dialog box. The interface also includes an Unwrap Only button. This button can be used to flatten the UVW Coordinates for the selected objects and to automatically create a map channel.

The General Settings rollout includes an output path where the baked texture is saved. The file is saved by default using the Targa file format. The Skip Existing Files option renders only those elements that don't already exist in the designated directory. The Rendered Frame Window option displays the resulting map in the Rendered Frame Window along with saving the image as a file. For the render pass, you can select which rendering settings to use, including the mental ray rendering engine. The Setup button opens the Render Scene panel, where you can change the render settings. In the Objects to Bake rollout a list displays exactly which objects, subobjects, and channels will be included in the rendered texture. The Edge Padding defines the overlap in pixels of the texture. The Projection Mapping section lets you enable the creation of a normal map using a Projection modifier. These settings are covered in detail in the Normal Map section that appears later in this chapter. The Mapping Coordinates section lets you choose to use the mapping coordinates of the Object or the Subobject selection contained within a specified channel or you can select to use the Use Automatic Unwrap feature, which automatically flattens the mapping coordinates. If the Use Automatic Unwrap option is selected, you can set the mapping options in the Automatic Mapping rollout. By default, unwrap mapping uses channel 3, but you can change this channel if you wish. If a different mapping uses channel 3 and you don't change this, the new mapping replaces the old one. The Clear Unwrappers button removes any existing Unwrap UVW modifiers from the object's stack. You can select to bake an Individual object, All Selected objects, or All Prepared objects, which are all objects with at least one texture element.

The Output rollout lists the texture elements that are included in the texture map. The Enable option can be used to disable the selected texture element or elements can be deleted with the Delete button. Clicking the Add button lets you select the type of texture elements that you can render. You'll want to use different maps depending on the purpose of the map, and you may want to render several at a time. The available types are CompleteMap, SpecularMap, DiffuseMap, ShadowsMap, LightingMap, NormalsMap, BlendMap, AlphaMap, and HeightMap. You can also change the map size or use the Automatic Map Size option, which bases the map size on the object size. Some map elements present a list of components to include in the map. These components appear below the size settings. The Baked Material and Automatic Mapping rollouts provide a way to keep the existing object material using the Shell material. The Clear Shell Materials button removes the Shell materials for the baked objects and restores their original materials. In the Automatic Mapping rollout, you can set how the mapping is applied. If the Use Automatic Unwrap option in the Objects to Bake rollout is enabled, then the object to be baked has the Automatic Flatten UVs modifier applied. For this type, you can set the Threshold Angle (which is the difference between the normals of adjacent faces; if the angular value is greater than the Threshold Angle value, then a hard edge is created between the faces), the Spacing (which is the amount of space between different map pieces), and whether map pieces can be rotated and used to fill in holes of larger map pieces. The size of the texture map depends on the size of the object, but you can set a Scale value for greater resolution and set Min and Max values to keep the maps within reason. By default, maps are saved to the /images directory, but you can select a different directory if you prefer. The Nearest Power of 2 option causes the map to be optimized for use in memory to a square pixel size that is a power of 2, such as 8 × 8, 16 × 16, 32 × 32, or 64 × 64.

Assigning vertex colors

Vertex colors can be assigned in the Surface Properties rollout for Editable Mesh and Editable Patch objects, and in the Vertex and Polygon Properties rollouts for Editable Poly objects. They also can be assigned in Face, Polygon, and Element subobject modes using a little rollout section called Edit Vertex Colors. Within this section are two color swatches for selecting Color and Illumination values. The Alpha value sets the alpha transparency value for the vertex.

Lesson 25
Working with Cameras

The cameras are used in Max to get custom views of a scene behave in many respects just like real-world cameras. It can offer many kinds of amusing views of your scene. The benefit of cameras is that you can position them anywhere within a scene to offer a custom view. You can open camera views in a viewport, and you can also use them to render images or animated sequences which can be animated as well. In the Camera Parameters rollout is a section for enabling Multi-Pass Camera Effects. These effects include Motion Blur and Depth of Field. Essentially, these effects are accomplished by taking several rendered images of a scene and combining them with some processing.

Max and real-world cameras both work with different lens settings, which are measured and defined in millimeters. You can select from a variety of preset stock lenses, including 35mm, 80mm, and even 200mm. Max cameras also offer complete control over the camera's focal length, field of view, and perspective for wide-angle or telephoto shots. The big difference is that you never have to worry about focusing a lens, setting flashes, or loading film. Light coming into a camera is bent through the camera lens and focused on the film, where the image is captured. The distance between the film and the lens is known as the focal length. This distance is measured in millimeters, and you can change it by switching to a different lens. On a camera that shoots 35mm film, a lens with a focal length of 50mm produces a view similar to what your eyes would see. A lens with a focal length less than 50mm is known as a wide-angle lens because it displays a wider view of the scene. A lens longer than 50mm is called a telephoto lens because it has the ability to give a closer view of objects for more detail, as a telescope does. Field of view is directly related to focal length and is a measurement of how much of the scene is visible. It is measured in degrees, as the shorter the focal length, the wider the field of view. When we look at a scene, objects appear larger if they are up close than they would be lying at a farther distance. This effect is referred to as perspective and helps us to interpret distances. As mentioned, a 50mm lens gives a perspective similar to what our eyes give. Images taken with a wide field of view look distorted because the effect of perspective is increased.

Creating a camera object

To create a camera object, you can use the Create> Cameras menu, or you can open the familiar Create panel and click the Cameras category button. The two types of cameras that you can create are a Free camera and a Target camera. Camera objects are visible as icons in the viewports, but they aren't rendered. The camera icon looks like a box with a smaller box in front of it, which represents the lens or front end of the camera. Both the Free and Target camera types can include a cone that shows where the camera is pointing. The Free camera object offers a view of the area that is directly in front of the camera and is the better choice if the camera will be animated. When a Free camera is initially created, it points at the negative Z-axis of the active viewport. The single parameter for Free cameras defines a Target Distance—the distance to an invisible target about which the camera can orbit. A Target camera always points at a controllable target point some distance in front of the camera. Target cameras are easy to aim and are useful for situations where the camera won't move. To create this type of camera, click a viewport to position the camera and drag to the location of its target. The target can be named along with the camera. When a target is created, Max automatically names the target by attaching ".target" to the end of the camera name. You can change this default name by typing a different name in the Name field.

You can change any viewport to show a camera's viewpoint. To do so, right-click the viewport's title, and select View and the camera's name from the pop-up menu. Any movements done to the camera are reflected immediately in the viewport. Another way to select a camera for a viewport is to press the C key. This keyboard shortcut makes the active viewport into a camera view. If several cameras exist in a scene, then the Select Camera dialog box appears, from which you can select a camera to use. You can turn off the camera object icons using the Display panel. In the Display panel, under the Hide by Category rollout, select the Cameras option. When selected, the camera icons are not visible in the viewports. Remember that cameras are usually positioned at some distance away from the rest of the scene. Their distant position can make scene objects appear very small when the Zoom Extents button is used. If the visibility of the camera icons is turned off, Zoom Extents does not include them in the zoom. You can also enable the Ignore Extents option in the camera's Object Properties dialog box.

Positioning a camera in viewport

I can understand your excitement to jump up and start playing around with cameras. But before you do anything, you've to get to know the procedure of it. First you have to draw or model something good in the viewport, then with the viewport selected you'll go to Create> Camera> Target Camera and you have to draw the camera facing the object of the viewport.

You can put one or more than one camera in any of the four viewports. To see the camera view, you can select the viewport and press C, and to go out of camera view right-click on viewport's name> Views> select viewport type. If anytime you think the viewport is messed up and you want to start all over again, go to File> Reset.

(1) For this tutorial, let's create a wheel with Tube of Standard Primitives. Draw a tube in the viewport and rotate it up. You can set Radius 1 to 40, Radius 2 to 15, and Height to 30.
(2) Select Create> Cameras> Target Camera, and drag in the viewport to create the camera making the target point and position correct. Then give the camera the name if you want
(3) If you put the camera in Perspective viewport, then having it selected press C on keyboard. It will open a camera view. The picture 6.2 A shows normal (without camera) view of the wheel in which the camera is just drawn, and the picture B shows its camera view. Save this file as wheel.max.

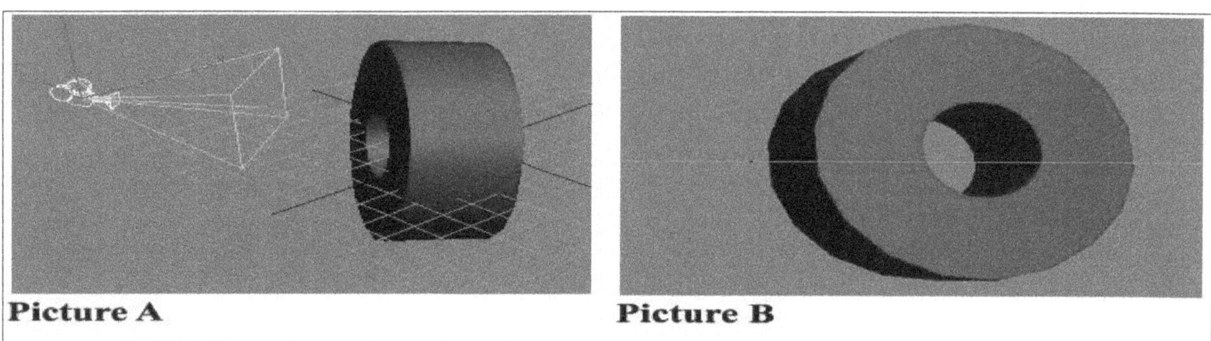

Picture 6.2 A and B

You control the camera view in a viewport by means of the Camera Navigation controls located in the lower-right corner of the screen. These controls replace the viewport controls when a camera view is selected and are different from the normal Viewport Navigation controls. You can constrain the movements to a single axis by holding down the Shift key. The Ctrl key causes the movements to increase rapidly. For example, holding down the Ctrl key while dragging the Perspective tool magnifies the amount of perspective applied to the viewport. You can undo changes in the normal viewports using the Views> Undo (Shift+Z) command, but you undo camera viewport changes with the regular Edit> Undo command. Using the Select and Rotate (E) button changes the direction in which a camera points, but only Free cameras rotate in all directions. When applied to a Target camera, the rotate transformation spins only the camera about the axis pointing to the target. You aim Target cameras by moving their targets.

Set target for a Target Camera in Animation
Surprises don't end in Max. The next surprise is that you can select the target for a Target camera by selecting its camera object, right-clicking to open the pop-up menu, and selecting Select Target. Because cameras can be transformed like any other geometry, they can also be set to watch the movements of any animation. This technique is applied in 3D movies that the people like to watch wearing 3D glasses.

(1) Open the same wheel.max file of previous tutorial in Max and delete the camera that you had created. In case you cannot go out of camera mode, do reset by File> Reset and create a new wheel.
(2) Move the wheel to the far right of Perspective viewport and select Create> Cameras> Target Camera, and drag in the viewport to create a small camera on the far left side. Set the Field of View (FOV) value to 100 degrees. The corresponding Lens value is around 1031mm.
(3) Now to select the camera target, click the Select and Link button in the main toolbar, and drag from the target to the wheel object. Press C to go to Camera view.
(4) Now press Auto Key N, and drag Time Slider to 100. Using Rotate tool you can rotate the wheel a little and press N again to exit key mode.
(5) Go to Animation> Make Animation> Create to see what happens. Remember the words of Einstein: Imagination is greater than knowledge.

Camera Parameters
In Camera Parameters rollouts you saw some buttons lens settings and field of view. The Orthographic Projection option displays the camera view in a manner similar to any of the orthographic viewports such as Top, Left, or Front. This eliminates any perspective distortion of objects farther back in the scene and displays true dimensions for all edges in the scene. Professional photographers and film crews use

standard stock lenses in the course of their work. These lenses can be simulated in Max by clicking one of the Stock Lens buttons. Preset stock lenses include 15, 20, 24, 28, 35, 50, 85, 135, and 200mm lengths. The Lens and FOV fields are automatically updated on stock lens selection.

As already said, you can position more than one camera in the same viewport, and with the camera object selected, if you go to Modify> Multi-Pass Effect rollout> Enable check of Motion Blur, you'll have motion blur in your animation.

Lesson 26
Lighting Techniques

Light play an important part in the visual process as in the 3D world it figures into every rendering calculation. Most Max scenes typically use one of two types of lighting: natural light or artificial light. Natural light is used for outside scenes and uses the sun and moon for its light source. Artificial light is usually reserved for indoor scenes where light bulbs provide the light. However, when working with lights, you'll sometimes use natural light indoors, such as sunlight streaming through a window, or artificial light outdoors, such as a streetlight. Natural light is best created using lights that have parallel light rays coming from a single direction: You can create this type of light using a Direct Light. The intensity of natural light is also dependent on the time, date, and location of the sun: You can control this intensity precisely using Max's Sunlight or Daylight systems. But artificial light is typically produced with multiple lights of lower intensity. The Omni light is usually a good choice for indoor lighting because it casts light rays in all directions from a single source. And the other lights like standard white fluorescent lights usually have a light green or light blue tint. When lighting a scene, don't rely on a single light because if you want to highlight a specific object, additional lights are needed. A good lighting method includes one key light and several secondary lights.

When you draw anything, Max places default lighting in the scene. But if you want to put light, first you create an object in the viewport, then go to Create> Lights and select and drag any light from the list in your viewport, but don't forget to render at the end. For example, you can try Create> Lights> Photometric Lights> Free Linear and place it at the bottom of your object.

Lighting a lamp

Picture 6.3

(1) First we have to create a wall. Go to Create> AEC Objects> Wall, pick up red color and draw a wall of three sides. Then go to Standard Primitives> Plane and draw a white color plane at the bottom.

(2) Now for the lamp, select Cone from Standard Primitives, pick up black color and draw it in the front viewport. Draw (in front viewport) a black Tube of Radius 1 value of 4 and Radius 2 value of 3 and place it as a stand of the lamp.

(3) Select the Create> Lights> Standard Lights> Omni menu command, and click in any viewport. Use the Move tool to position the light object inside the lamp's light bulb. When you render the scene, it should look like the picture 6.3.

Like this, you can create many effects using other lighting options. Lights effects make the image real and viewable. Gear up your imagination and surprise yourself with *surpasses*!

Shadow parameters

All light types have a Shadow Parameters rollout that you can use to select a shadow color by clicking the color swatch. The default color is black. The Dens setting stands for "Density" and controls how dark the shadow appears. Lower values produce light shadows, and higher values produce dark shadows. This value can also be negative. The Map option, like the Projection Map, can be used to project a map along with the shadow color. The Light Affects Shadow Color option alters the Shadow Color by blending

it with the light color if selected. In the Atmosphere Shadows section, the On button lets you determine whether atmospheric effects, such as fog, can cast shadows. You can also control the Opacity and the degree to which atmospheric colors blend with the Shadow Color. When you select a light and open the Modify panel, one additional rollout is available: the Atmospheres and Effects rollout. This rollout is a shortcut to the Environment dialog box, where you can specify atmospheric effects such as fog and volume lights. The picture 6.4 can give you an idea of the shadow.

Picture 6.4

For the Shadow Map option, the Shadow Map Params rollout includes values for the Bias, Size, and Sample Range. The Sample Range value softens the shadow edges. You can also select to use an Absolute Map Bias and 2 Sided Shadows. If the Ray Traced Shadows option is selected in the Shadow Parameters rollout, the Ray Traced Shadows Parameters rollout appears below it. This simple rollout includes only two values: Bias and Max Quadtree Depth. The Bias settings cause the shadow to move toward or away from the object that casts the shadow. The Max Quadtree Depth determines the accuracy of the shadows by controlling how long the ray paths are followed. There is also an option to enable 2 Sided Shadows.

Using the Compass helper

The Compass helper is useful when working with a Sunlight system. It can be used to define the map directions of North, East, South, and West. The Sunlight system uses these directions to orient the system light. This helper is not renderable and is created automatically when you define a sunlight object. After you create a Sunlight system, you can alter the sun's position by transforming the Compass helper. Doing so causes the direct light object to move appropriately. You cannot transform the Direct light by itself.

Understanding Azimuth and Altitude

Azimuth and Altitude are two values that help define the location of the sun in the sky. Both are measured in degrees. Azimuth refers to the compass direction and can range from 0 to 360, with 0 degrees being North, 90 degrees being East, 180 degrees being South, and 270 degrees being West. Altitude is the angle in degrees between the sun and the horizon. This value ranges typically between 0 and 90, with 0 degrees being either sunrise or sunset and 90 when the sun is directly overhead.

Using Volume Lights

When light shines through fog, smoke, or dust, the beam of the light becomes visible. The effect is known as a Volume Light. To add a Volume Light to a scene, choose Rendering> Environment (or press the 8 key) to open the Environment dialog box.

Then click the Add button in the Atmosphere rollout to open the Add Atmospheric Effect dialog box, and select Volume Light. The parameters for the volume light are presented in the Volume Light Parameters rollout. You can also access the Volume Light effect from the Atmospheres and Effects rollout in the Modify panel when a light is selected. At the top of the Volume Light Parameters rollout is a Pick Light button, which enables you to select a light to apply the effect to. You can select several lights, which then appear in a drop-down list. You can remove lights from this list with the Remove Light button. In the Volume section, the Fog Color swatch lets you select a color for the fog that is seen within the light. This color is combined with the color of the light. The Attenuation Color is the color the fog appears to have at a distance far from the light source. This color also combines with the Fog Color and is best set to a dark color. The picture 6.5 shows Volume Lights.

Picture 6.5

Lesson 27
Learning Animation
It is animation that motivates a great majority of people to learn Max. In today's world everyone wants to create something for moving visual expression. Max includes many different tools to create animations and one of them is—keyframe animation, which works on Time Controls located on the lower interface bar between the key controls and the Viewport Navigation Controls. The Time Controls also include the Time Slider found directly under the viewports. The Time Slider provides an easy way to move through the frames of an animation. To do this, just drag the Time Slider button in either direction. The Time Slider button is labeled with the current frame number and the total number of frames. The arrow buttons on either side of this button work the same as the Previous and Next Frame (Key) buttons. The Time Control buttons include buttons to jump to Start or End of the animation, or to step forward or back by a single frame. You can also jump to an exact frame by entering frame number in the frame number field. The default scene starts with 100 frames, but this is seldom what you actually need. You can change the number of frames at any time by clicking the Time Configuration button, which is to the right of the frame number field. Clicking this button opens the Time Configuration dialog box. You can also access this dialog box by right-clicking any of the Time Control buttons.

Setting frame rate
Within this dialog box, you can set several options, including the Frame Rate. Frame rate provides connection between the number of frames and time. It's measured in frames per second. The options include standard frame rates such as NTSC (National Television Standards Committee, around 30 frames per second), Film (around 24 frames per second), and PAL (Phase Alternate Line, used by European countries, around 25 frames per second), or you can select Custom and enter your own frame rate. Time Display section lets you set how time is displayed on the Time Slider. Options include Frames, SMPTE (Society of Motion Picture Technical Engineers), Frame:Ticks, or MM:SS:Ticks (Minutes and Seconds). SMPTE is a standard time measurement used in video and television. A Tick is 1/4800 of a second.

The Playback section sets options for how the animation sequence is played back. The Real Time option skips frames to maintain the specified frame rate. The Active Viewport Only option causes the animation to play only in a single viewport, which speeds up the animation. The Loop option repeats the animation over and over. The Loop option is available only if the Real Time option is disabled. If the Loop option is set, then you can specify the Direction as Forward, Reverse, or Ping-Pong (which repeats playing forward and then reverse). The Speed setting can be 1/4, 1/2, 1, 2, or 4 times normal. The Time Configuration dialog box also lets you specify the Start Time, End Time, Length, and Current Time values. These values are all interrelated, so setting the Length and the Start Time, for example, automatically changes the End Time. These values can be changed at any time without destroying any keys. For example, if you have an animation of 500 frames and you set the Start and End Time to 30 and 50, the Time Slider controls only those 21 frames. Keys before or after this time are still available and can be accessed by resetting the Start and End Time values to 0 and 500. The Re-scale Time button fits all the keys into the active time segment by stretching or shrinking the number of frames between keys. You can use this feature to resize the animation to the number of frames defined by Start and End Time values. The Key Steps group lets you set which key objects are navigated using key mode. If you select Use Track Bar, key mode moves through only the keys on the Track Bar. If you select the Selected Objects Only option, key mode jumps only to the keys for the currently selected object. You can also filter to move between Position, Rotation, and Scale keys. The Use Current Transform option locates only those keys that are the same as the current selected transform button.

Working with Keys

Creating and working with keys is how animations are accomplished. Keys define a particular state of an object at a particular time. Animations are created as the object moves or changes between two different key states. Complex animations can be generated with only a handful of keys. You can create keys in numerous ways, but the easiest is with the Key Controls found on the lower interface bar. These controls are located to the left of the Time Controls. Picture 6.6 shows all the keys with their description.

Toolbar Button	Name	Description
	Set Keys (K)	Creates animation keys in Set Key mode.
Auto Key	Toggle AutoKey Mode (N)	Sets keys automatically for the selected object when enabled.
Set Key	Toggle Set Key Mode (')	Sets keys as specified by the key filters for the selected object when enabled.
Selected ▼	Selection Set drop-down list	Specifies a selection set to use for the given keys.
	Default In/Out Tangents for New Keys	Assigns the default tangents that are used on all new keys.
Key Filters...	Open Filters Dialog box	Contains pop-up options for the filtering keys.

Picture 6.6

Max includes two animation modes: Auto Key (N) and Set Key ('). You can select either of these modes by clicking the respective buttons at the bottom of the interface. When active, the button turns bright red, and the border around the active viewport also turns red to remind you that you are in animate mode. Red also appears around a spinner for any animated parameters.

Auto Key mode

With the Auto Key button enabled, every transformation or parameter change creates a key that defines where and how an object should look at that specific frame. To create a key, drag the Time Slider to a frame where you want to create a key and then move the selected object or change the parameter, and a key is automatically created. When the first key is created, Max automatically goes back and creates a key for frame 0 that holds the object's original position or parameter. Upon setting the key, Max then interpolates all the positions and changes between the keys. The keys are displayed in the Track Bar. Each frame can hold several different keys, but only one for each type of transform and each parameter. For example, if you move, rotate, scale, and change the Radius parameter for a sphere object with the Auto Key mode enabled, then separate keys are created for position, rotation, scaling, and a parameter change.

Set Key mode

The Set Key button (') offers more control over key creation and sets keys only when you click the Set Key button (K). It also creates keys only for the key types enabled in the Key Filters dialog box. You can open the Key Filters dialog box by clicking the Key Filters button. Available key types include All, Position, Rotation, Scale, IK Parameters, Object Parameters, Custom Attributes, Modifiers, Materials, and Other (which allows keys to be set for manipulator values).

Using trajectories

A trajectory is the actual path that the animation follows, in other words, it allows you to see the animation path as a spline. When you click the Trajectories button in the Motion panel of Command

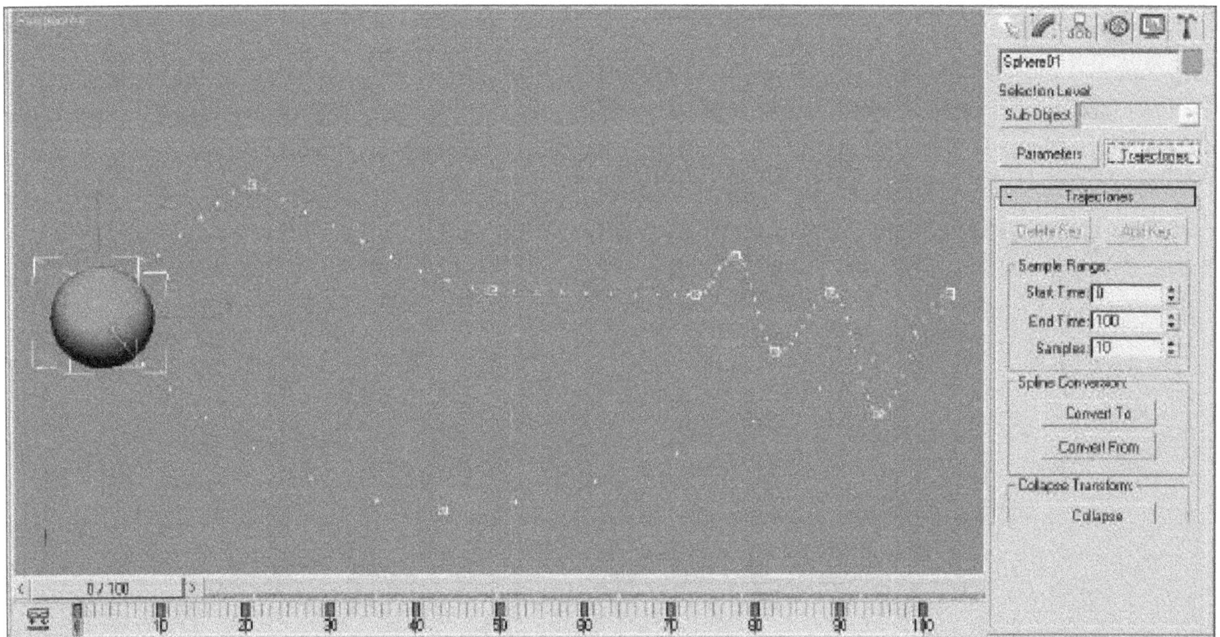

Picture 6.7

panel, the animation trajectory is shown as a spline with each key displayed as a node and each frame shown as a white dot. You can then edit the trajectory and its nodes by clicking the Sub-Object button at the top of the Motion panel, shown in picture 6.7. The only subobject available is Keys. With the Sub-Object button enabled, you can use the transform buttons to move and reposition the trajectory nodes. You can also add and delete keys with the Add Key and Delete Key buttons. For more control over the trajectory path, you can convert the trajectory path to a normal editable spline with the Convert To button.

Creating or deleting keys in the Time Slider
Another way to create keys is to select the object to be animated and right-click the Time Slider button. This opens the Create Key dialog box where you can set Position, Rotation, and Scale keys for the currently selected object. You can use this method only to create transform keys. If you want to delete all object animation keys, remember that individual keys can be selected and deleted using the Track Bar (which is situated directly under the Time Slider), or the right-click pop-up menu, but if an object has many keys, you can choose Animation> Delete Selected Animation menu command.

Using Ghosting
Ghosting displays a copy of the object being animated before and after its current position. This feature is very helpful in creating animation as it lets you know where your current object should be placed. To enable ghosting, choose Views> Show Ghosting. This command uses the options set in the Preference Settings dialog box. You can access this by choosing Customize> Preferences. In the Viewports panel of this dialog box is a Ghosting section. You use this Ghosting section to set how many ghosted objects are to appear; whether the ghosted objects appear before, after, or both before and after the current frame; and whether frame numbers should be shown. You can also specify every Nth frame to be displayed. You also have an option to display the ghost object in wireframe (they are displayed as shaded if this option is not enabled) and an option to Show Frame Numbers. Objects before the current frame are colored yellow, and objects after are colored light blue.

Creating Animation Previews
You create previews by choosing Animation> Make Preview to open the Make Preview dialog. In the Make Preview dialog box, you can specify what frames to include using the Active Time Segment or Custom Range options. You can also choose Every Nth Frame or select a specific frame rate in the Playback FPS field. The image size is determined by the Percent of Output value, which is a percentage of the final output size. The resolution is also displayed. The Display in Preview section offers a variety of options to include in the preview. These options include Geometry, Shapes, Lights, Cameras, Helpers, Space Warps, Particle Systems, Active Grid, Safe Frames, Frame Numbers, Background, and Bone Objects. Because the preview output is rendered like the viewports, certain selected objects such as Lights and Cameras actually display their icons as part of the file. The Frame Numbers option prints the frame number in the upper-left corner of each frame.

Output options include the default AVI option; a Custom File Type option, which enables you to choose your own format; and the Use Device option, which you can use to render the preview to a different device. For the AVI option, you can select a CODEC, which is used to compress the resulting file. Options include Cinepak Code by Radius, Microsoft Video 1, and Full Frames (uncompressed), depending on the CODECs that are installed on your system. When the Use Device option is selected, the Choose Device button becomes active. Clicking this button opens the Select Output Image Device dialog box, where you can select and configure output devices such as a Digital Recorder.

Using Sound Options dialog box

To apply sound, first you have to complete your animation, then in the beginning of the Time Frame (at the bottom of the left viewport corner) click on Track View button. To find this button, if you place mouse pointer on it, it says 'Open Mini Curve Editor'. You can click on it to expand animation setting box. In that animation setting box click on + sign of Sound option. Then double-left click on Metronome to activate and right-click on it again and select Properties. In Sound Options Properties you can click Choose Sound button. Picture 6.8 shows Sound Options dialog box.

The Sound Options dialog box lets you select a sound to play during the animation. You can make the sound track appear as a waveform curve under the Track Bar. This helps as you try to synchronize the sound to the movements in the viewports. If you want to see this sound track, you can right-click the Track Bar, and choose Configure> Show Sound Track from the pop-up menu. You can use the Audio section of the Sound Options dialog box to load a sound or remove an existing sound.

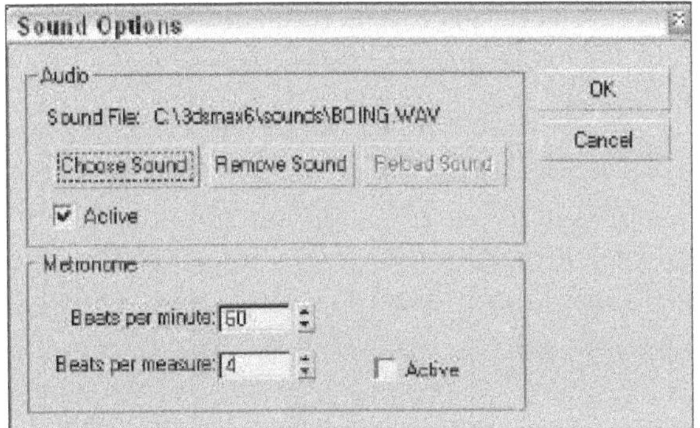

Picture 6.8

The Active option causes the sound file to play when the animation is played. The Choose Sound button can load AVI, WAV, and FLC file types. The dialog box also includes buttons to Remove Sound and Reload Sound. You can also set up a regular metronome beat with two tones. For a metronome, you can specify the beats per minute and the beats per measure. The first option sets how often the beats occur, and the second option determines how often a different tone is played. This dialog box also contains an Active option for turning the metronome on and off.

Lesson 28
Working with Characters

Now this lesson is going to give you a feeling of perfection in learning Max. You must have seen many 3D characters in movies. Using Biped (Create> Systems> Biped), you can create a fully linked and constrained human-form skeleton by simply dragging in the viewport. Biped objects can be altered in

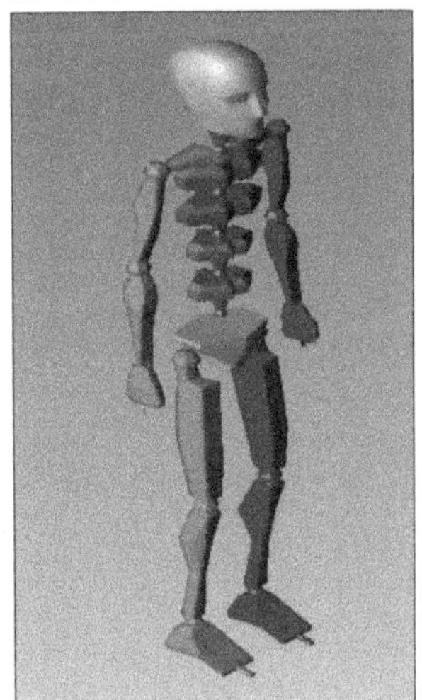

many ways while retaining their benefit. The major benefit of bipeds is that you can realistically animate them by simply positioning their footprints or setting freeform keys. Max includes many other features for rigging characters which you'll learn in this lesson, but if you plan on animating a character that walks on two legs and has two arms, then biped is definitely the way to go.

(1) To create a biped, simply select the Create> Systems> Biped and drag in a viewport. The Biped menu command accesses the Biped button found in the Systems category of the Create panel. The Create Biped rollout includes two creation methods: Drag Height and Drag Position. The picture 6.9-1 shows the Biped image. In the Create Biped rollout, there are several links for Neck, Tail and other body parts that can be changed by entering number if you are structuring an animal. Right now you don't need to do that.

Picture 6.9-1

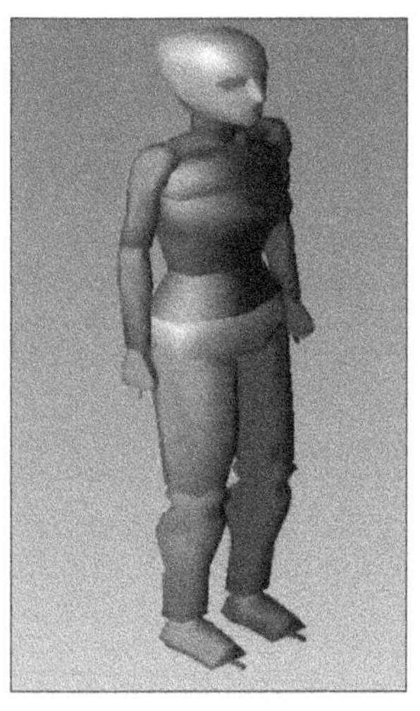

(2) Below the Biped Name field is the Body Type drop-down list. In this list, you can select from Skeleton, Female, Male, and Classic body types. I have selected the option Female for the picture 6.9-2 below. The moment I selected Female in the drop-down list, the character changed to a slightly thinner shape with apparent female body. But this is not the end; we have a lot more to do.

The differences among these body types relate to the size and shape of the bones. By default, all biped bones are color coded, with all bones on the right side colored green and all bones on the left side colored blue. The pelvis, which is the root bone, is colored yellow, and the head is light blue.

These colors help keep the different bones straight, and the same colors are used for the footprints that define the biped's motion. The standard biped resembles a human form but you can use the settings in the Create panel to radically change the biped to resemble whatever creature you've created.

Picture 6.9-2

Customized biped skeletons can be saved using the Save File button found in the Motion panel when Figure Mode is enabled. Biped files are saved with the .fig file extension. Saved biped files can then be recalled when a new biped is being created using the Open Fig File button in the Create Biped rollout. The Create Biped rollout also includes settings for toggling the arms on and off. Settings are available for controlling the number of links used to represent all the various body parts. These same settings are available in the Structure rollout of the Motion panel, which is available when Figure Mode is enabled. After a biped is created, you may look to the Modify panel to change the biped, but the Modify panel is empty. Don't be surprised: All the controls for modifying a biped are located in the Motion panel. This is because biped deals with animation and not just with modifying structures. In the Biped rollout of the Motion panel, you see several icons that are used to modify structures.

(3) If you perform this step (step 3), it'll create a skin for the character making the entire skin a single object and retain its materials. Till now you have the female character on your screen which looks similar to one shown in picture 6.9-2. Now go ahead and select the pelvis object of the character, and convert it to an Editable Poly object using the right-click quadmenu. In the Modify panel that opens, click the setting dialog box button next to the Attach button in the Edit Geometry rollout. The Attach List dialog box opens. Click the All button to select all objects, and then click the Attach button. In the Attach Options dialog box that appears, choose the Match Material to Material IDs option and click the OK button. I am sure you would like it, but remember that if your system configuration is low, then Max may encounter a problem and it will be closed. If the problem persists, do not perform this step or try on the other computer.

(4) After creating skin you can enable animation (press N) and drag the Time Slider to 100. Then open the Motion panel, and click the Figure Mode button in the Biped rollout to enter Figure Mode. In the Bend Links rollout, click the Bend Links Mode button and bend the structure the way you want, and exit out of animation mode. Let me tell you one thing that you may have a hard time moving the structure after creating skin because the entire skin is a single object. If you don't succeed at all, then you can skip step 3.

Using Footstep Mode

When you want a biped to make animated walk, there are two modes that you can use: Footstep Mode and Freeform Mode. Both have advantages. Footstep Mode is useful for characters that need to walk, run, or jump. It ensures that the feet stay parallel to the ground at all times and can be used to walk over rough terrain. Freeform Mode doesn't constrain the biped and is used for all other actions. Footstep Mode is enabled by clicking the Footstep Mode button in the Biped rollout of the Motion panel. This button turns light yellow when enabled and opens several additional rollouts. The easiest way to create footsteps is to click the Create Footsteps (at current frame) button in the Footstep Creation rollout and then click in the viewport where the footprints are to be located. By default, the left foot is placed first and the footprints alternate between right and left. Left footprints are marked in blue, and right footprints are marked in green. Until keys are created, you can select, move, and rotate footsteps.

These footprints can be positioned anywhere within the scene, and the biped automatically creates the motion required including all the realistic secondary motion such as swinging arms. You can also select to have the biped be running or jumping using the buttons in the Footstep Creation rollout. Using the Walk Footstep and Double Support values located under the Walk button, you can set how quickly the footstep animation happens. The Walk Footstep value is the number of frames for which the foot remains within the footstep, and the Double Support value is the number of frames during which both feet are touching the ground.

Making a biped jump on a box

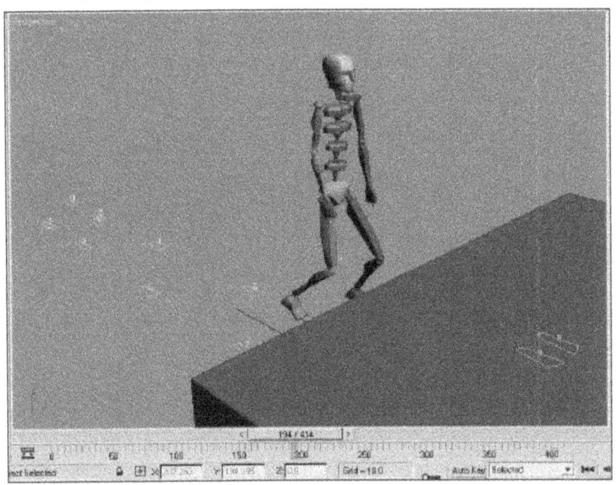

(1) Create a box and biped in your viewport. Be sure to leave enough room between the biped and the box so the biped can get a running start.

(2) Open the Motion panel, and click the Footstep Mode button in the Biped rollout to enter Footstep Mode. In Footstep Creation rollout, select the Walk button and click the Create Footsteps button. Then click in the viewport to create four footsteps in front of the biped object starting with the right foot.

(3) Choose the Run option in the Footstep Creation rollout, select the Create Footsteps (append) button, and add four more steps that are spread out slightly more than first steps (see picture 7.0).

Picture 7.0

(4) Choose the Jump option in the Footstep Creation rollout, and click the Create Multiple Footsteps button. In the Create Multiple Footsteps dialog box that opens, set the Number of Footsteps to 2, and click the OK button. The two footsteps where the biped lands that should be in the center of the box object.

(5) Select and move the final two footsteps upward in the Left viewport to be on top of the Box object.

(6) Click the Create Keys for Inactive Footsteps button in the Footstep Operations rollout to create the keys for the available footsteps. Click the Play Animation button to see the biped walk, run, and jump on the box.

If you're looking for the ways to save Max animation to play in a different video player, then go to Animation> Make Animation> Create. When it starts playing the video in an auto-enabled player, there you can click on File> Save Video. There is one more thing important to say that you can directly drag and drop still image (JPEG file) to Perspective viewport.

Making a puppet using bones

(1) Select Create> Systems> Bones IK Chain, and in the IK Chain Assignment rollout, select IK Limb from the IK Solver drop-down list. To be able to see the orientation of each bone, enable the Side Fins.

(2) In the Front viewport, click where you want the head bone to start and click again where the neck will be, and then continue to click to form the spine, pelvis, right thigh, right lower leg, and foot bones. At the end you can right-click to end the bones chain.

(3) While still in Bones mode, click the pelvis bone in the Front viewport and drag to the left to form the left thigh bone. Continue to click to form left lower leg and left foot bones, and right-click to end chain.

(4) Form the right arm bones by clicking the head bone and clicking consecutively to form the right

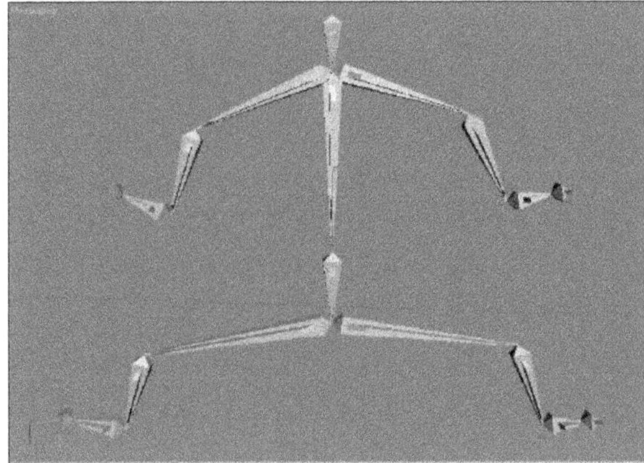

upper arm, right lower arm, and hand bones. You can right-click to end the chain.

(5) Repeat Step 4 for the left arm.

(6) Click the Select Objects button on the main toolbar to exit Bones mode, and select and name each bone object so it can be easily identified later. Picture 7.1 shows the completed bones system for the puppet. You can select the bone at the end of each chain and move it to see how the inverse kinematics solution works. You can do the step 3 of Working with Characters chapter (page 69) to create skin for these bones, but one bone at a time.

Picture 7.1

Lesson 29
Saving animations

Biped animations are saved to the hard disk as .bip files using the Save File button found in the Biped rollout. This opens a Save As dialog box. For the animation sequence, you can select the range of frames to save. For .bip files, you also can save additional Max objects and controllers with the file, such as a target object that the head follows. The Save File button in the Biped rollout may be used to save .FIG, .BIP, and .STP files, but only .BIP files save the motion information that can be loaded into the Motion Mixer. FIG files save only the structure and position of the biped, and STP files save footstep timing and location data, but no keys.

In addition to biped animation sequences, the animation of other objects also can be saved using the XML Animation File (XAF) format. You can save the animation for the selected object, open the Save XML Animation File dialog box using the File> Save Animation File. For general animations, you can select to include tracks, constraints, only keyable tracks, and a specific range. The User Data fields let you enter notes or specific data used by plug-ins about the animation sequence. Within the Character Assembly rollout for Character objects is a button to Save Animation. This button saves character animations using the ANM file format, which cannot be opened using the File> Load Animation menu command. The Viewport Background can load animation clips, which can make positioning characters to match real motion easy. But as already said, before an animation sequence can be reused, it first must be saved in a format that Max can load again. Max supports files saved as XML Animation Files (XAF) using the File> Save Animation File menu command.

Using Motion Mix

If you've worked to animate a biped or some other Max object and are pleased with the result, you can save the animation clip and reuse it. Several animation clips can be mixed together to create an entirely new animation sequence. The Motion Mixer lets you add several different animations to the interface comprising both biped and non-biped objects. The animations then can be blended and transitioned between the loaded animation clips. You also can modify clips as needed. Before an animation sequence can be mixed in the Motion Mixer, it must be saved. The Motion Mixer easily can load any existing animation sequence in the current opened Max file, but saving a sequence to the local hard disk makes it accessible for other Max scenes. The Motion Mixer can be accessed using the Graph Editors> Motion Mixer menu command.

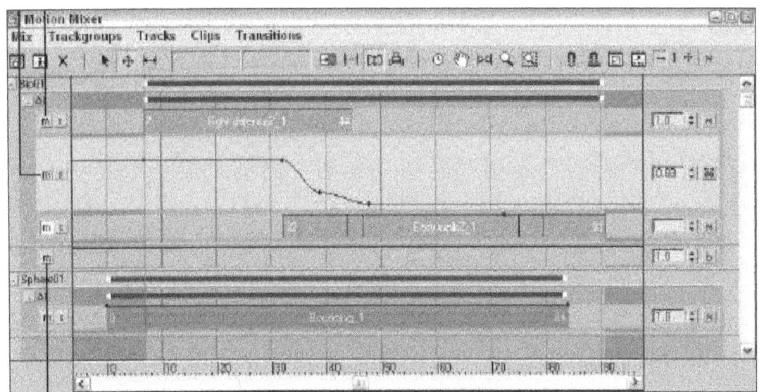

Picture 7.2

The Motion Mixer is a completely separate interface. The same interface also is opened using the Mixer button found in the Biped Apps rollout of the Motion panel when a biped is selected. If the Mixer button is used, then the Motion Mixer opens with the biped already added as a track to the mixer interface. Picture 7.2 shows the Motion Mixer interface with each loaded animation on a separate track.

Creating a Space Warp

You can think of Space Warps as the unseen forces that control the movement of objects in the scene such as gravity, wind, and waves. Several Space Warps, such as Push and Motor, deal with dynamic simulations and can define forces in real-world units. Space Warps are not renderable and must be

Picture 7.3

bound to an object to have an effect. Some Space Warps can deform an object's surface; others provide the same functionality as certain modifiers. Space Warps are found in the Create> Space Warps menu, which opens the Space Warps category (the icon is three wavy lines) in the Create panel. From the subcategory drop-down list, you can select from four different subcategories. Each subcategory has buttons to enable several different Space Warps, or you can select them using the Create> Space Warps menu command. Now to create it, click a button or select a menu option and then click and drag in a viewport. You can use Space Warps on Scatter objects as well as particle systems, shown in picture 7.3.

When a Space Warp is created, a gizmo is placed in the scene. This gizmo can be transformed as other objects can: by using the standard transformation buttons. The size and position of the Space Warp gizmo often affects its results. After a Space Warp is created, it affects only the objects to which it is bound.

Using reactor

'reactor' brings a wow factor in Max as it is a complex piece of software with a huge assortment of features that enable you to define physical properties and forces and have the scene automatically generate the resulting animation keys as the objects interact while following the laws of physics. The reactor plug-in interface exists in the Utilities panel and is one of the default utilities, but you can also access it from the reactor menu and the reactor toolbar, shown in picture 7.4. The reactor menu and the reactor toolbar provide a quick and easy way to access the various reactor elements. For example,

clicking the Rope Collection button opens the Helper category in the Command Panel, selects the reactor subcategory, and selects the RP Collection button.

Picture 7.4

Reactor works with geometry that is defined with certain physical properties. After these properties are defined, the reactor engine can take over and determine how all the various objects interact with one another. Defining geometry with physical properties happens in several different ways. Objects can be added to a collection. A collection is a type of reactor object that has several inherited physical properties such as a Rigid Body collection. Objects can also be linked with reactor objects such as a Spring or Motor. These objects are affected by forces that are preset for the different reactor objects. Finally, you can set properties using the Object Property rollout that lets you define properties such as mass, friction, and elasticity. After all the objects are defined and attached to the correct reaction collection or object, you can open a Preview window that lets you see how the object will react under the current forces. You can also interactively play with the various objects in the Preview window. The command, reactor> Create Animation creates all the keys for the animation sequence. Reactor can be used to simulate cloth falling realistically over a chair, a monster truck moving up and over the hill, and so on.

Adding motion effect using reactor

We are tying to animate a bunch of marbles using reactor. If you were using keyframes, determining

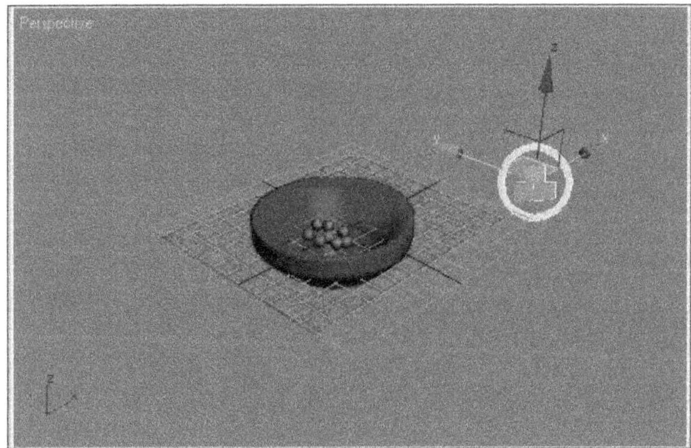

whether an object overlaps another would be difficult, but with this quick example, we see the power of reactor.

(1) Draw a green Plane in Perspective viewport which should look like a floor. In Front viewport, draw a blue color bowl. To draw the bowl you can use the steps (first way) mentioned in the lesson: <u>Creating trumpet flowers</u> of page 43. See picture 7.5 for help.

(2) Use Sphere to draw some red marbles. You'll use Front view because you want the marbles to be above the bowl.

Picture 7.5

(3) Select reactor> Create Objects> Rigid Body Collection, and click in the Front viewport to create the icon. In the RB Collection Properties rollout, click the Add button to open the Select Objects dialog box.

(4) In the Select Objects dialog box, click the All button and then the Select button to select and make all objects in the scene rigid body objects. Then right-click on Rigid Body Collector button and select Close to exit this mode.

(5) Select the bowl and floor objects, select reactor> Open Property Editor, and enable the Unyielding option. This prevents these two objects from moving. Then select the sphere bowl object, and enable the Concave Mesh option.

(6) Select all the marble objects in the scene, and set the Mass value to 5.0. Then select reactor> Preview Animation to open the Preview window, and press the P key to start the simulation.

7. If the animation looks fine, select reactor> Create Animation to have reactor compute all the keys. After it is done, you can select Animation> Make Animation.

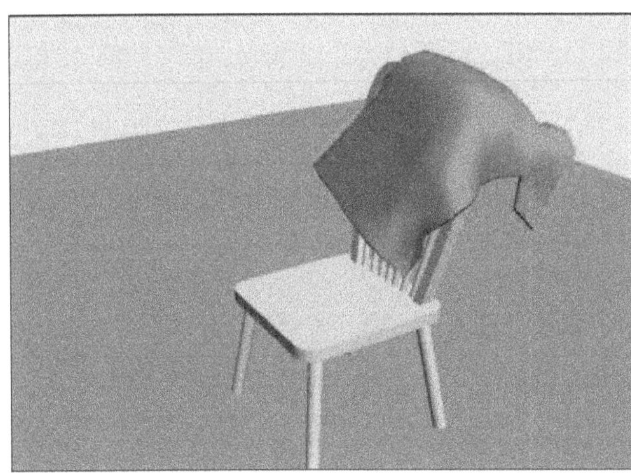

Picture 7.6

In reactor, the simulation identifies the various objects by the type of collection that it is part of it. Reactor has five types of collections (Toolbar Buttons) — Rigid Body, Cloth, Soft Body, Rope, and Deforming Mesh. (A) Rigid Body Collection resists a force. (B) Cloth Collection makes 'flow and bend' the object with all forces. (C) Soft Body Collection flexes when they come in contact with a force. (D) Rope Collection ropes objects support tension, but not compression. (E) Deforming Mesh Collection can be deformed by forces. Reactor can be used to simulate cloth falling realistically over a chair, see picture 7.6.

Lesson 30
Rendering and mental ray
After modeling, applying materials, positioning lights and cameras, and animating your scene, you're finally ready to render the final output. The Rendering menu is the doorway to the final output. The Render command (F10) opens the Render Scene dialog box where you can set output options such as which frames to render and the final image size. The Environment command (keyboard shortcut, 8) opens the Environment dialog box where you can specify the environment settings such as a background color or image, global lighting settings, and atmospheric effects such as Combustion, Fog, and Volume Lights. The Effects command opens the Rendering Effects dialog box. You use the Rendering Effects dialog box to add rendered effects to an image without having to use the Video Post dialog box. The Effects categories include options such as Lens Effects, Blur, and Color Balance. The Advanced Lighting command opens a control panel where the settings for the Light Tracer, Radiosity, Exposure Control, and Lighting Analysis tools are located.

The Render to Texture command (keyboard shortcut, 0) allows you to render the current scene as an image to be used as a texture. The Batch Render command opens an interface where you can specify several projects to render unattended. The Raytracer Settings command opens a dialog box for enabling raytracing options, and the Raytrace Global Include/Exclude command opens a dialog box where you can specify which objects are rendered using raytracing and which are not. The mental ray Message Window opens a window where you can view error and status messages produced by the mental ray rendering engine. The ActiveShade Floater opens the ActiveShade window, where you can get immediate rendered results. The ActiveShade Viewport command displays the immediate rendered results in the active viewport. The Material Editor (keyboard shortcut, M) and Material/Map Browser commands open their respective dialog boxes for creating, defining, and applying materials. The Video Post command opens a dialog box for scheduling and controlling any post-processing work. The dialog box manages events for compositing images and including special effects such as glows, lens effects, and blurs. The Show Last Rendering command immediately recalls the last rendered image produced by the

Render command. The Panorama Exporter command allows you to render a panoramic scene. The Print Size Wizard is a godsend for anyone who is printing images from Max. It relates the current scene to the common paper sizes that printers use. The RAM Player can display images and animations in memory and includes two channels for overlaying images and comparing animations side by side.

The Render Output section enables you to output the image or animations to a file, a device, or the Rendered Frame Window. To save the output to a file, click the Files button and select a location in the Render Output File dialog box. Supported formats include .AVI, .BMP, .DDS, Postscript (.EPS), JPEG, Kodak Cineon (.CIN), Open EXR, .FLC, Radiance Image File (.HDRI), QuickTime (.MOV), .PNG, .RLA, .RPF, SGI's Format (.RGB), Targa (.TGA), and .TIF. The Device button can output to a device such as a video recorder. If the Rendered Frame Window option is selected, then both the Files and Devices buttons are disabled. You also have an option to Put Image File List in Output Path, which creates a list of image files in the same location as the rendered file. You also have the choice of choosing Max's IFL standard or the Autodesk ME Image Sequence File (IMSQ). The Create Now button creates an image list instantly.

Creating Atmospheric Effects
Max includes dialog boxes for setting the color, background images, and lighting environment; these features can help define your scene. This chapter covers atmospheric effects, including the likes of clouds, fog, fire, and volume lights. These effects can be seen only when the scene is rendered. The Environment and Effects dialog box (keyboard shortcut, 8) contains rollouts for adding atmospheric effects to your scene, but the first question is where. Atmospheric effects are placed within a container called an Atmospheric Apparatus gizmo, which tells the effect where it should be located. However, only the Fire and the Volume Fog effects need Atmospheric Apparatus gizmos. To create an Atmospheric Apparatus gizmo, select Create> Helpers> Atmospherics and choose the apparatus type. The three different Atmospheric Apparatus gizmos are BoxGizmo, SphereGizmo, and CylGizmo. Each has a different shape similar to the primitives.
When working with the Atmospheric Apparatus, selecting a gizmo and opening the Modify panel reveals two different rollouts: one for defining the basic parameters such as the gizmo dimensions, and another labeled Atmospheres & Effects, which you can use to Add or Delete an Environment Effect to the gizmo. Each gizmo parameters rollout also includes a Seed value and a New Seed button. The Seed value sets a random number used to compute the atmospheric effect, and the New Seed button automatically generates a random seed. Two gizmos with the same seed values have nearly identical results.

Enabling mental ray
As a renderer, mental ray is very fast. It also includes support for global illumination without having to enable the Advanced Lighting settings. In addition, mental ray can use all of Max's existing materials without having to use a limited specialized material like the Raytrace material. Each material has a new rollout that lets you specialize mental ray settings. Mental ray also includes native support for Area Lights, Shaders, Depth of Field, and Motion Blur. It also includes some specialized lights that offer functionality, such as caustics, that are unavailable in the Scanline Renderer. To choose mental ray as the renderer for your scene, simply select it from the list of available renderers in the Assign Renderer rollout of the Common panel of the Render Scene dialog box. You can set a different renderer for Production, the Material Editor, and the ActiveShade viewer. To make mental ray your default renderer, click the Save as Defaults button in this rollout. Once selected as your Production renderer, you don't need to modify any other settings for the renderer to work. The mental ray settings in the Material Editor, Lights category, and Object Properties dialog box enable additional features that mental ray can take advantage of, but they aren't required to render the scene.

In the Preference Settings dialog box is a panel of global mental ray settings. In this panel, you can select to enable mental ray Extensions. These extensions add some additional controls to several of the various mental ray panels. When the Scanline Renderer renders a scene, it progresses one line of pixels at a time down the image, but mental ray renders the image by breaking it up into blocks and rendering a block at a time. The Show Brackets on Current Buckets option displays white brackets around the current block as the image renders. You can also select to clear the frame before rendering. The Messages section lets you specify which messages are displayed as the file renders. Options include Errors, Log Information, Log Progress, Debug Messages, and whether to write this information to a file. The mental ray renderer also includes many additional features that you can take advantage of, including Depth of Field, Motion Blur, Contours, Displacement, and Camera Shaders. The settings for these additional features are located in rollouts at the bottom of the Renderer panel.

Automating with MAXScript

Though Max's has a wide range of capabilities, yet there may come a time when you wish for a new Max feature. With MAXScript, you can actually extend Max to meet your needs, customize it to work the way you want, and even have it do some of the more monotonous tasks for you. MAXScript is a tool that you can use to expand the functionality of Max. You can use it to add new features or to customize how Max behaves, so that it's tailored to your needs and style. It can also record your actions so you can play them back later, eliminating repetitive tasks. It is easy to use and was designed from the ground up to be an integral part of Max. As a language, it is rich enough to let you control just about anything. In fact, you have already used MAXScript without even knowing it. Some of the buttons and rollouts use bits of MAXScript to carry out your commands. And after you've created a new feature with MAXScript, you can integrate it into Max transparently and use it just as easily as any other Max feature. It is a fully functional and very powerful computer language, but you don't have to be a computer programmer or even have any previous programming experience to benefit from it. MAXScript is so powerful that an entire book could be written about it, but that is not the purpose here. This chapter is organized to give you an introduction to the world of MAXScript and to teach you the basic skills you need to get some mileage out of it. What is given here is a foundation that you can build upon according to your own interests and needs.

```
SphereArray.ms - MAXScript
File  Edit  Search  Debugger  Help
utility sphereArray "Sphere Array"
(
spinner objCount "Object count:" range:[1,100,20] type:#integer
spinner radius "Radius:" range:[1,1000,50]

button go "Go!"

on go pressed do
(
  a = selection[1]
  if a != undefined do
  (
    c = objCount.value
    r = radius.value
    for i = 1 to c do
    (
      someObj = copy a
      someObj.position.x = someObj.position.x + r
      about selection rotate someObj (random 0 359) x_axis
      about selection rotate someObj (random 0 359) y_axis
      about selection rotate someObj (random 0 359) z_axis
    )
  )
)
)
```

Picture 7.7

The MAXScript menu includes commands that you can use to create a new script, open and run scripts, open the MAXScript Listener window (keyboard shortcut, F11), enable the Macro Recorder, open the Visual MAXScript Editor, or access the Debugger dialog box.

The New Script command opens a MAXScript editor window, a simple text editor in which you write your MAXScript. See the "MAXScript editor windows" section later in this chapter for more on this editor window. The Open Script command opens a file dialog box that you can use to locate a MAXScript file. When opened, the script file is opened in a MAXScript editor window. MAXScript files have an .MS or .MCR extension. The Run Script command also opens a file dialog box where you can select a script to be executed. Picture 7.7 shows the MAXScript Editor.

MAXScript Commands

When you use Run Script, some scripts do something right away, whereas others install themselves as new tools. To start using MAXScript, follow these steps:

(1) Choose File> Reset to reset Max.

(2) Choose MAXScript> MAXScript Listener (or press F11) to open the MAXScript Listener window, shown in picture 7.8.

(3) Click anywhere in the bottom pane of the Listener window, type the following, and press Enter:

sphere()

A sphere object with default parameters is created.

(4) Next enter the following in the lower pane, and press the Enter key:

torus radius1:50 radius2:5

Max creates a torus and adds it to your scene. As you specified in your MAXScript, the outer radius (radius1) is 50, and the radius of the torus itself (radius2) is 5. The output tells you that Max created a new torus at the origin of the coordinate system and gave that torus a name: Torus01.

(5) Now use MAXScript to move the torus. In the Listener window, type the following:

$Torus01.position.x = 20

After you press Enter, you see the torus move along the positive X-axis. Each object in Max has certain properties or attributes that describe it, and what you've done is access one of these properties programmatically instead of by using the rollout or the mouse. In this case, you're telling Max, "Torus01 has a position property. Set the Xcoordinate of that position to 20." The $ symbol identifies a named object. You can use it to refer to any named object.

(6) To see a list of some of the properties specific to a torus, type the following:

Showproperties $Torus01

A list of the Torus01 properties appears in the window. Picture 7.8 shows the MAXScript Listener window with all the associated commands, and the picture 7.9 shows the results. An important thing to

Picture 7.8

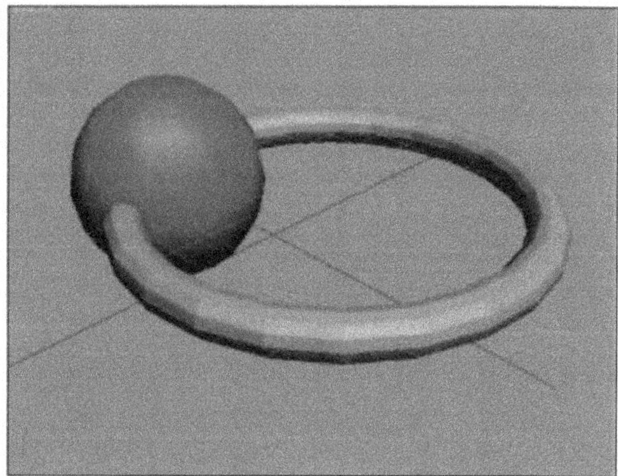

Picture 7.9

understand from this tutorial is that you can do almost anything with MAXScript. Any property of any object that you can access via a rollout is also available via MAXScript. You could go so far as to create entire scenes using just MAXScript, although the real power comes from using MAXScript to do things for you automatically. At the left end of the status bar, you can access the MAXScript Mini Listener control by dragging the left edge of the status bar to the right. By right-clicking in this control, you can open a Listener window and view all the current commands recorded by the Listener.

Niranjan Jha Showman
Trainer, Author, Physician, Entrepreneur, Filmmaker, Activist
Cromosys Corporation
Education and Technology Research Center
www.facebook.com/cromosys
+91-9561450045
Nallasopara (W), Mumbai, India

NIRANJAN JHA SHOWMAN

Founder - Niranjan Jha Showman

Education and Technology Research Center

Patankar Park, Nallasopara (W), Mumbai. +91-9561450045

Education, Technology, Publication, Healthcare, Newsmedia, Realtor, Filmmaking

www.facebook.com/cromosys

Cromosys Publication
Teach
Yourself
German
NIRANJAN JHA SHOWMAN

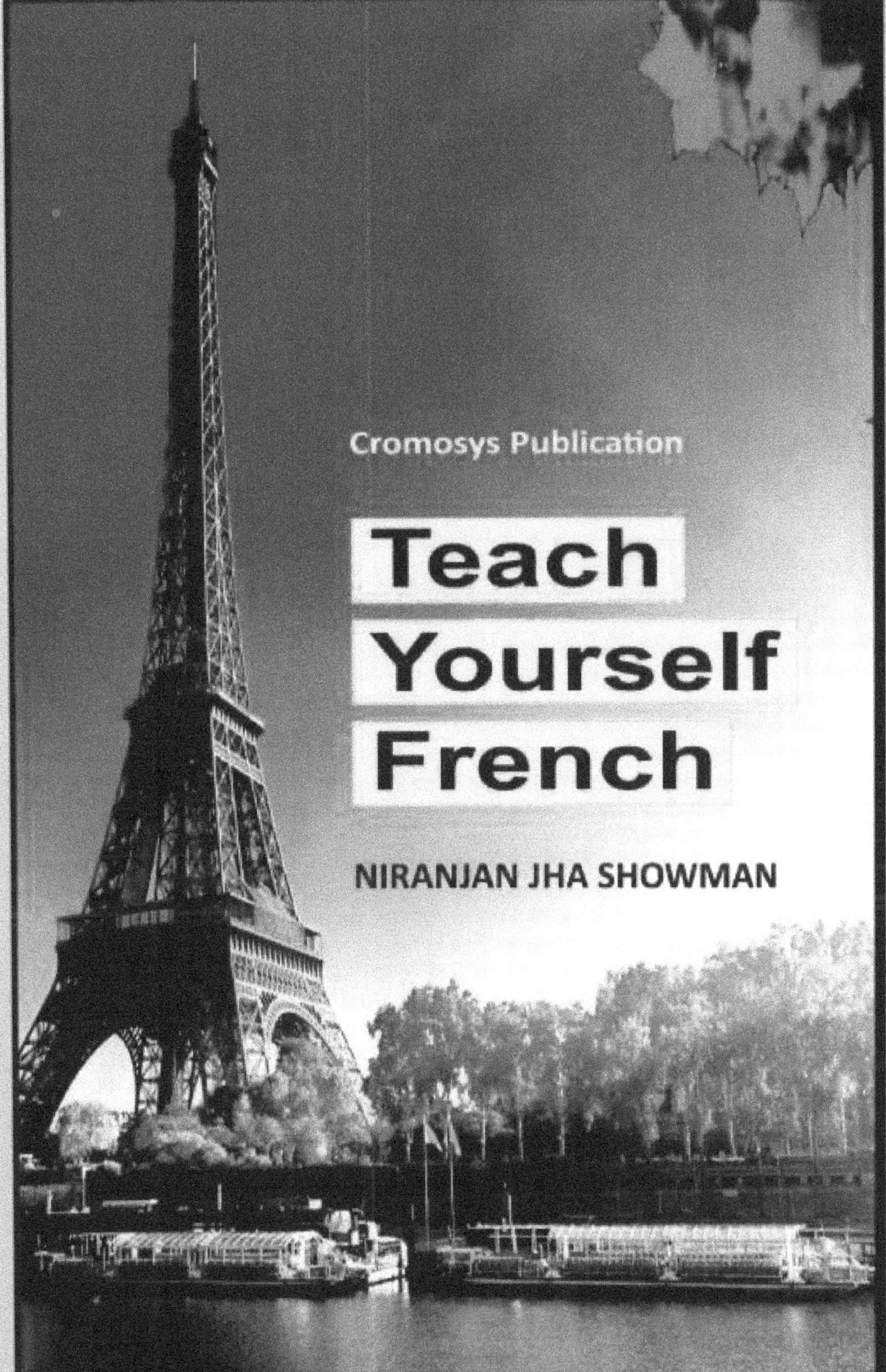

Cromosys Publication
Teach
Yourself
French
NIRANJAN JHA SHOWMAN

Cromosys Publication
Teach
Yourself
Spanish
NIRANJAN JHA SHOWMAN

Cromosys Publication

English
Voice
Accent and
Pronunciation

NIRANJAN JHA SHOWMAN

Teach
Yourself
Autodesk
MAYA
Cromosys Publication
NIRANJAN JHA SHOWMAN

Cromosys Publication
Teach
Yourself
Autodesk
3ds Max
NIRANJAN JHA SHOWMAN

Cromosys Publication
CRIMINAL FACTORY
NIRANJAN JHA SHOWMAN

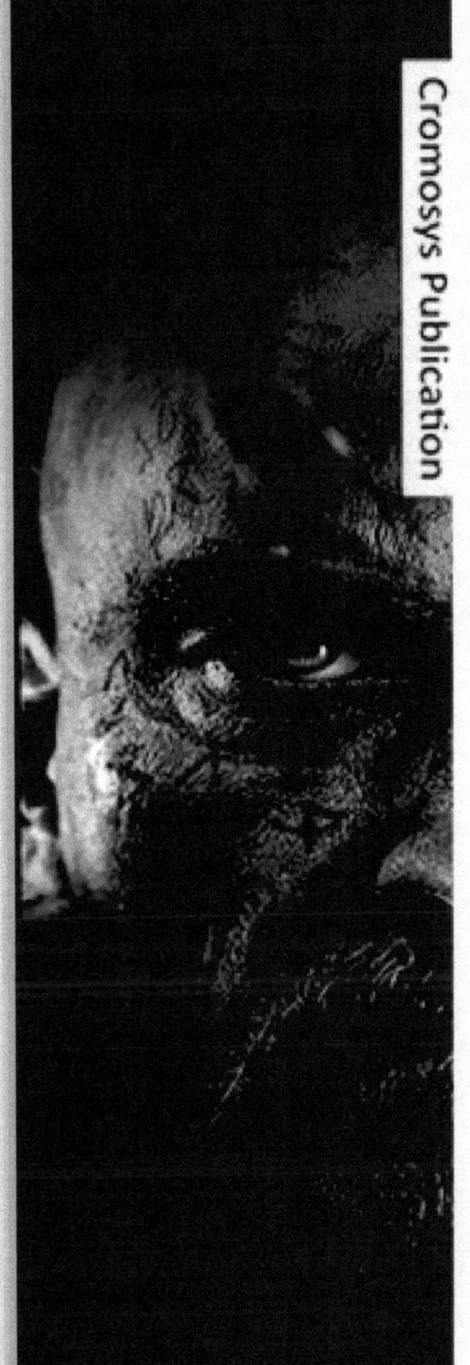
Cromosys Publication
FOCAL DISASTER
NIRANJAN JHA SHOWMAN

Cromosys Publication
Your talents will not help you succeed without your skill of using them.
NIRANJAN JHA SHOWMAN
BE
MILLIONAIRE
LIKE
ME

Copyright Office
Government of India

सत्यमेव जयते

Extracts
from the Register
of Copyrights

Dated : 22/07/2022

1.	Registration Number	: **T -86768/2022**
2.	Name, address and nationality of the applicant	: NIRANJAN JHA SHOWMAN, CROMOSYS PUBLICATION, 001, JAYSATYAM, PATANKAR ROAD, NALLASOPARA (W), MUMBAI, MAHARASHTRA - 401203. INDIAN
3.	Nature of the applicant's interest in the copyright of the work	: AUTHOR
4.	Class and description of the work	: LITERARY / BOOK
5.	Title of the work	: **Teach Yourself Autodesk 3ds Max**
6.	Language of the work	: ENGLISH
7.	Name, address and nationality of the author and if the author is deceased, date of his decease	: NIRANJAN JHA SHOWMAN, CROMOSYS PUBLICATION, 001, JAYSATYAM, PATANKAR ROAD, NALLASOPARA (W), MUMBAI, MAHARASHTRA - 401203. INDIAN
8.	Whether the work is published or unpublished	: UNPUBLISHED
9.	Year and country of first publication and name, address and nationality of the publisher	: N.A.
10.	Years and countries of subsequent publications, if any, and names, addresses and nationalities of the publishers	: N.A. SAME AS ABOVE
11.	Names, addresses and nationalities of the owners of various rights comprising the copyright in the work and the extent of rights held by each, together with particulars of assignments and licences, if any	:
12.	Names, addresses and nationalities of other persons, if any, authorised to assign or licence of rights comprising the copyright	: N.A.
13.	If the work is an 'Artistic work', the location of the original work, including name, address and nationality of the person in possession of the work. (In the case of an architectural work, the year of completion of the work should also be shown).	: N.A.
14.	If the work is an 'Artistic work', whether it is registered under the Designs Act 2000 if yes give details.	: N.A.
15.	If the work is an 'Artistic work', capable of being registered as a design under the Designs Act 2000.whether it has been applied to an article though an industrial process and ,if yes ,the number of times it is reproduced.	: N.A.
16.	Remarks, if any	:

Diary Number :   5396/2020-CO/N
Date of Application : 05/05/2020
Date of Receipt :   05/05/2020

DEPUTY REGISTRAR OF COPYRIGHTS

Cromosys Publication

Teach Yourself Autodesk 3ds Max

NIRANJAN JHA SHOWMAN

www.ingramcontent.com/pod-product-compliance
Lightning Source LLC
Chambersburg PA
CBHW040147110726
48005CB00018B/2684